A People's History of Psychoanalysis

"An absolutely fascinating book."

—*Lundimatin*

"A reminder of the discipline's historical links with the struggle for emancipation and against social inequalities."

—*France Culture*

"Psychoanalyst Florent Gabarron-Garcia ... re-establishes his practice in a narrative other than the one that claims not to be involved in politics."

—*L'Écho*

A People's History of Psychoanalysis

Florent Gabarron-Garcia

Translated by Shuli Branson

First published as *Histoire populaire de la psychanalyse* in 2021 by La Fabrique Éditions
First English language edition published 2025 by Pluto Press
New Wing, Somerset House, Strand, London WC2R 1LA
and Pluto Press, Inc.
1930 Village Center Circle, 3-834, Las Vegas, NV 89134

www.plutobooks.com

This book is supported by the Institut français (Royaume-Uni) as part of the Burgess programme.

Copyright © La Fabrique Éditions, 2021, 2025

English language translation copyright © Shuli Branson 2025

The right of Florent Gabarron-Garcia to be identified as the author of this work has been asserted in accordance with the Copyright, Designs and Patents Act 1988.

British Library Cataloguing in Publication Data
A catalogue record for this book is available from the British Library

ISBN 978 0 7453 4960 2 Paperback
ISBN 978 0 7453 4958 9 PDF
ISBN 978 0 7453 4959 6 EPUB

This book is printed on paper suitable for recycling and made from fully managed and sustained forest sources. Logging, pulping and manufacturing processes are expected to conform to the environmental standards of the country of origin.

Typeset by Stanford DTP Services, Northampton, England

Simultaneously printed in the United Kingdom and United States of America

EU GPSR Authorised Representative
LOGOS EUROPE, 9 rue Nicolas Poussin, 17000, LA ROCHELLE, France
Email: Contact@logoseurope.eu

Contents

List of Figures   viii

Introduction   1
  Towards a Political History of Psychoanalysis   1
  Psychoanalysis: The New Watchdog?   5

1. Freud Looks East: Vera Schmidt and Psychoanalysis in the Land of the Soviets   10
  Freud and the Communist Hypothesis   10
  Freud and Other Analysts' Commitment to Practice   17
  The Sexual Revolution and Psychoanalysis in the Russian Revolution   22
  The Psychoanalysis of Children and Education in Revolutionary Russia   26
  Practice in the Children's Home   29

2. Wilhelm Reich: From the Vienna Policlinic to the Sexpol in Berlin   34
  The Clinical Foundations of Reich's Political Commitment: The Policlinic   34
  Reich's Seminar at the Policlinic   37
  The Poor Patients of the Vienna Policlinic   41
  Reich's Fragment of an Analysis of a Working Woman   45
  Taking Social Deprivation into Account in the Determination of Neuroses and Their New Therapeutic Needs   47

Prevention of Neurosis and Communist Militancy   50
Clinical Experience in the Sexual Hygiene Centers and the Critique of Science   55
The Disagreement with Freud   62
Sexual Repression and the Critique of the Communist Party   66
The Politicization of Sexual Life and the Success of Sexpol   71

3. The Future of Freudian Pessimism   77
   The Context of Freud's Reversal: The End of the Hope in Russia and the Rise of Nazism   78
   Ernest Jones, The "Savior" of Psychoanalysis   82
   What Nazism Did to Psychoanalysis: Eitingon's Departure   84
   "Neutrality" in Psychoanalysis and Aryanization of the German Psychoanalytic Society   90

4. Marie Langer: From 1930s Vienna to 1970s Latin America   100
   Marie Langer's Resistance in 1930s Vienna   100
   Early Years   102
   Impossible Neutrality   105
   The International Brigades in Spain   108
   The Need for Self-Censorship in the Psychoanalytic Association   110
   Political Reawakening   112
   Plataforma Argentina and New Psychoanalytic Praxis   116
   The New Psychoanalytic Clinic in Avellaneda   119
   The Shutdown by the Dictatorship and the "Neutrality" of Psychoanalysis   124

5. From the Catalonian Commune to La Borde Clinic — 126

Tosquelles and the 1930s in Catalonia — 126
The Context of the Spanish Revolution — 128
Tosquelles's Therapeutic Action during the War — 131
The Model of the Comarcas — 133
From Sept-Fons to Saint-Alban — 135
The Post-War Context in France and the Founding of La Borde — 139
Political and Clinical Stakes — 144
Analysis in Psychiatry — 147
The Revolution Achieved by Psychoanalysis — 153
The Question of Group Fantasy in Guattari — 156
The Object of Psychoanalysis: From the objet petit "a" ... — 161
... to the "objet b" — 166

6. Revival of Revolutionary Psychoanalysis in Germany: The Heidelberg Experience — 169

The Political Context of the SPK's Birth — 170
The Theoretical Constellation of the SPK — 172
Reich among the Doctors — 175
Partial Drive, Exchange Value, and Illness — 177
Political Critique of the Healthcare System as Ideological Apparatus — 181
Patient Power and Proletarian Power — 184
Repression — 189

Conclusion: For Another Psychoanalysis — 193

Notes — 199
Index — 235

Figures

1	Vera Schmidt	28
2	Wilhelm Reich, circa 1943	38
3	Sigmund Freud, G. Stanley Hall, Carl Gustav Jung, Abraham A. Brill, Ernest Jones and Sándor Ferenczi	79
4	Marie Langer	104
5	François Tosquelles, Jean Oury and Gisela Pankow in Milan in 1975	141
6	Félix Guattari	159
7	In the SPK group meeting room, September/October 1970	171

Introduction

Towards a Political History of Psychoanalysis

The myth of a neutral psychoanalysis is completely misleading. The strength and fruitfulness of politicized psychoanalysis proves this, whether in the 1920s—largely "forgotten" today even though supported by Freud himself—or in the 1970s, generally regarded with contempt but connected to the earlier era. But even beyond these two paradigmatic times, we will show that a political view is in fact integral to psychoanalysis, including—perhaps above all—when it claims to escape politics and founders in psychoanalism.

As shocking as it might seem for many analysts today, Freud defended a progressive, optimistic political vision *in practice*, even one sympathetic to communism at least until 1927.[1] This vision was widespread among analysts;[2] it was pursued by many of them long after Freud. In the 1920s, the little-known cutting-edge experiment of Vera Schmidt and her home for children in Bolshevik Russia, which revolutionized the psychoanalysis of children, drew great interest for Freud and his collaborators. Schmidt's work had no equivalent in western Europe and served as an example for many analysts.

In this book, we will also look back at the career of Wilhelm Reich. Far from the cliched views that relegate him to the sidelines, his position in the 1920s linked him with the prestigious third generation of analysts, whose members all demonstrated an intense political engagement.[3] For a long time, Freud supported these young analysts, who, eager and not yet benefitting from private clientele, invested in a clinical practice geared towards the poorest people.

We will see that the "disavowal" of Reich in 1929—which proponents of psychoanalytic pessimism endlessly champion—was actually part of a major theoretical shift by Freud. Beyond the case of Reich, in a deteriorating geopolitical context, this turn created a new practical focus that put the majority of analysts in a quandary. It had serious consequences for international psychoanalysis—in hindsight, even more serious than the disastrous promotion during the same years of Aryan psychology by Carl Jung,[4] the most repulsive figure in the orthodox history.

Against this Freudian reversal, the career of Marie Langer, who got her start at the beginning of the 1930s, is, in our view, pivotal for the destiny of psychoanalysis. Marxist, feminist, communist, and young, as a psychoanalyst, she was committed to revolutionary action. Like Reich, she remained convinced that the three fronts of psychoanalysis, Marxism, and feminism formed a unified struggle. We will follow her career from Red Vienna to Argentina, by way of the International Brigades in Spain.[5]

Another long and instructive chain of events for our history revolves around François Tosquelles. Trained in Catalonia by the Red Vienna psychoanalysts exiled by the war, he took up the cause of the Catalonian commune, before revolutionizing the Saint-Alban hospital in France.

La Borde Clinic, founded in 1953 by Oury (and soon joined by Guattari), is part of his legacy.

Finally, we will discuss the revitalization of German psychoanalysis in Heidelberg during the 1970s and the story of the "Socialist Patients Collective" (SPK). The revolutionary radicality of this experiment, like the state violence unleashed against it, echoes the tragic destiny of German psychoanalysis in the face of Nazism in the 1930s. Despite numerous works by historians, this story is still covered in silence in the psychoanalytic field.

The reader should understand that we have used a method which is the opposite of what we have learned in the Parisian "schools of psychoanalysis." Rather than a reading based in exegesis, we will open the texts to a historical reading. By shedding light on the networks and actual clinical and political practices of analysts in their historical context, while referring to certain foundational texts—by Freud, but not only him—we will see a whole other history of practices emerge, a history that allows for a new understanding of the texts and their interpretation.[6] Though this narrative may seem disparate and discontinuous, putting the various trajectories of analysis in their proper historical contexts will reveal the threads that bind them, whether in the form of strange traumatic repetitions that echo across time, space, and wars, or in the form of seemingly unique practical experiences that resonate with each other. Finally, we will try to show what connects us to, and what separates us from, these politicized moments of psychoanalysis today. The history we present here is above all *a history of possibilities*, which reinterprets the official narrative of our discipline in light of some of its decisive splits. The official French psychoanalytic history, the one taught in the university psychoanalysis departments or in the "schools" of psychoanalysis, generally neglects this history. In the end, it is a matter of shedding light on the present moment of the discipline in order to reopen and reconnect it to the sharpness of Freud's discovery.[7]

Of course, we must remember: the psychoanalytic couch is essentially a place of protest and speech, both of which came first from women. Freud's invention of the *talking cure* found its origin in his patients' protests against the medical order—represented overwhelmingly by men, who did not listen to them. Epilepsy, paralysis of the limbs, and hysteria did not have biological causes. As Freud argued, how can we deny that the flare of symptoms they suffered, like the inhibition to thinking that struck them, was tied to the social domination they endured and the repression they experienced from childhood? Decades later, during the Algerian war of independence, Frantz Fanon made a similar observation when several of his formerly colonized patients displayed symptoms of ulcers and deformities of the spine.[8] In psychoanalysis, this singular voice, which was initially silenced, seeks to be heard despite domination, denial, control, and perversion. And the analyst must quite often bear witness to a mute suffering without a name that can go as far as to seize control of the patient's body. Only the work of the cure can liberate the subject. This possibility for the subject to take their destiny back into their own hands, to open pathways that give voice to their desire, and to leave behind their belittlement—this is the promise opened by psychoanalysis. In the turmoil of contemporary domination, a time when the framework of "biological causation" threatens to return, we can show that the talking cure, because it has a revolutionary vision, remains invaluable for our age.

Psychoanalysis: The New Watchdog?

For decades, psychoanalysis has by and large been deeply and openly reactionary. Lately, the number of its retrograde stances has rapidly increased, reaching new heights of stupidity, ignorance, and bad faith.

It started with the frenzy around security and the stigmatization of "gangs of youths in uniform" who no longer respect "knowledge" or "authority."[9] With the advent of civil unions, followed by gay marriage, adoption by homosexual couples, and medically assisted reproduction, some analysts advanced theories which were echoed widely by the media: the very foundations of desire would be undermined and anthropological collapse would be close at hand. The questioning of "patricentric society," the recognition of homosexual desire, and the winning of new rights, would, according to them, signal the end of a "human presence on earth."[10] The promoters of this apocalyptic vision have found new confirmation in the recent social and political climate, which they have commented on abundantly. #MeToo and "indiscriminate neo-feminism", they say, want to create a sick society without order [*sans re-père*, without coordinates, without a father], the education of children would be doomed to failure and madness, and civilization would come to an end. Then it was the turn of the "gilet jaunes," the popular insurrection which they said was an expression of "infantile narcissistic omnipotence" and the "unleashing of the death drive." The state, they say, is weak and adrift, for too long it has lacked manly authority: the children of the "big mother" no longer understand the limits required for us to live together.[11] Topping this collection of stupidity, second only to gender studies,[12] is "intersectional" critique in the university that is truly responsible for the rise of the totalitarianism that threatens "Thought" and "Our Culture." At a time when racism infects the public realm, the cause of this evil ravaging our society and threatening implosion is not social inequality but rather the ideological grip of decolonial and/or postcolonial intellectuals and academics who promote communitarianism, which paves the way for totalitarianism.[13]

Under the pretext of boldness and having the courage to "confront political correctness," these positions, sometimes even claiming to be critiques of neoliberalism, all share, despite some differences, an opposition to real political equality. They are the testimony of a generation gone renegade.[14] Hostile and pedantic, vehemently opposed to winning new rights, culturally pessimistic, and anthropologically declinist, they hate political equality, which, according to some of them, expresses nothing less than a "death wish"![15] In their feverishness, they cannot bear that critique reveals the oppression exercised by their very world.[16]

The noise around this reactionary blossoming, however, is not so new. What is perhaps new is the media coverage and the power it has in public debate. Following the model of the New Philosophers, in the 1980s the neo-analysts began to produce a literature filled with hatred for history and progress, a vernacular that has flourished in the field of psychoanalysis—though at that time, still quietly. This set the ground for the reaction that was to come. These analysts systematically deny history, specifically any progressive and revolutionary history. They saw May 1968 as an anal regression.[17] But charity begins at home, as they say, and the analysts then applied this therapy to their own field. All politicized psychoanalysis was discredited. According to the champions of this tendency, "the dangerous political excess" of Deleuze and Guattari's *Anti-Oedipus*[18] and Wilhelm Reich had to be exposed.[19] These were merely "marginal" and "isolated figures"—and, besides, Freud himself "would have been shocked"[20] by the involvement of the French psychoanalytic movement in the uprisings of May 1968. The "unfortunate interlude of militancy" in the history of psychoanalysis was over.[21] Any Freudian-Marxist or progressive view was suspicious. Any egalitarian aim was simply a way to "deny the lack"—castration. In every case, they say, this dangerous approach, which is so inclined to deny the constitutive aggression of the sexual drive and the guilty anxiety innate to the human psyche, paves the way for totalitarianism. Therefore, psychoanalysis had to be "purified." Taking the "pure gold of psychoanalysis" as a self-evident truth,[22] they explained to students—including me—that the time had come to choose: either "the fantastical illusion of politics," or "the ethics of the Subject and its truth." Once "sobered up from these ideals," the psychoanalyst could no longer be (or ever have been) militant ... except as a psychoanalyst.[23]

Psychoanalysis had finally reached the "age of reason," thus changing the course of its studies. Soon hatred for history and for those struggling for emancipation, trapped in the law of an eternal unconscious Sameness, reached a new level in the treatment of the French Revolution, systematically linked to the Terror. This somewhat hackneyed move has been around since François Furet.[24] But even more than Furet, the theses of the neo-analysts excel in this most refined fallacy thanks to an infallible method: the Revolution is a simple oedipal story. The whole revolutionary timeline of 1789 now fits the oedipal narrative, presented as a *regression*[25]—in a striking infantilization of history and in spite of the facts. And recently the French Revolution has been related to the "desire for the death of the father."[26] The same aversion to the struggle for emancipation can equally be found in the treatment of current events: during the Arab Spring, some were quick to describe the desire expressed as a "desire for consumption," an individualist claim to a "right to pleasure" in consuming "the poisonous pleasures of the Accountable Individual and the Isolated Self on which Uncle Sam gorges himself."[27]

Enough with the bad examples. We must admit the sad fact: while the New Philosophers, like reactionary historians, have generally been dismissed and seem to be in decline, psychoanalysis appears to have replaced them in the role of the "new watchdog" of power. Clearly, guard duty is always taken up to defend anthropological arguments about the "structure of the psyche," which is assumed to take precedence over any social reality. And, following the paradox of what psychopathology calls perversion, while this discourse delivers its prejudices about men, women, and politics, and naturalizes aggression, it claims to do so in the name of a supposed political neutrality, whose privilege it alone holds. Like all bourgeois thought, this psychoanalysis believes to speak the truth about human nature beyond cultural and historical differences. Is this still psychoanalysis? It seems unlikely. This is why we propose to name it instead *psychoanalism*, a discourse that participates in domination and in the construction of ideology as the "production of ideas through which a dominant class justifies its domination."

In contrast to Robert Castel, whose term we borrow from the title of one of his books in the 1970s,[28] psychoanalism is not our principal object of study. Yet it is perhaps an original illness of our discipline. In the 1920s, the psychoanalyst Kolnai, in a "neutral manner," was quick to describe communism as a "regression to the mother."[29] And however far as one goes back in history of the discipline, depending on sociohistorical conditions more or less favorable to its development, psychoanalism seems to haunt the field of analytic practice and theory, either as a fleeting specter with little influence, or as an omnipotent monster towering over it. As someone trained in it, when I look over contemporary analytic literature—at least going back to the 1980s—I can only attest that until recently the discipline has been in the grip of the real Leviathan of psychoanalism. This book proposes to tear this to pieces—not making it the focus but, rather, suggesting a cure. Psychoanalism is surely a tendency inherent in our discipline, one of the possible distortions that condemn it to a dead end. It assumes a certain relationship to history, which it reifies, and from which we hope to free ourselves starting with our own disciplinary history.

1
Freud Looks East: Vera Schmidt and Psychoanalysis in the Land of the Soviets

Freud and the Communist Hypothesis

A certain hermeneutic orthodoxy often claims that a *cultural pessimism* is inherent in Freud's analytic theory. This view is generally based on one of his later books, *Civilization and Its Discontents*,[1] in which he unequivocally condemns communism: Repeating the Hobbesian maxim that "man is a wolf to man," Freud claims the repression stemming from civilization is a necessary and inevitable evil needed to master the strength of the individual's drives. Backed up by this reference, some analysts will go as far as to claim that there is no escaping it: "Evil" is inherent to Man.[2] Other analysts, less drunk on the metaphysics of Evil, develop more refined but no less problematic claims: The psychoanalyst must maintain an attitude of *political neutrality*. Ernest Jones, Freud's closest collaborator in the last part of his life and author of a monumental and still authoritative[3] hagiography of the master from Vienna, even reported that Freud, when accused that psychoanalysis was "neither black nor red, neither Fascist nor Socialist," responded, "No, one should be flesh coloured."[4] The master's position was thus supposedly "not having any bias." The dominant and conventional reading approaches the political dimension in all of Freud's work, and quite often by extension the whole of psychoanalysis itself, as pessimism or "indifferentism."[5]

But, as the reader will agree, such a reading is not innocuous. Not only does it fail to do justice to the nuances and evolution of Freud's thought, but, above all—and this is the subject of this book—it overlooks the reality of *psychoanalytic practices* in society that Freud himself initiated. Indeed, at the 1918 International Congress of Psychoanalysis in Budapest, Freud called to expand the reach of classical psychoanalysis, which up until that point had only reached the most affluent, to include the most impoverished. His wish for a people's psychoanalysis came true, as a dozen policlinics were set up throughout Europe after the congress. All the analysts in the largest capital cities of the time responded to his call: in Budapest, Berlin, Moscow, Vienna, Zagreb, London, Trieste, Rome, Frankfurt, and Paris. This undertaking had unmistakable and clearly stated political aims. These aims are even reflected in the spelling chosen for the policlinics: Preferring the "i" of politics to the "y" evoking the variety of treatments, the name clearly signified political commitment to the city. The psychoanalyst therefore could not be less indifferent, and psychoanalysis was far from being neutral.

But it does not mean that these analysts were "lone revolutionaries," nor did they belong to the "vanguard." The whole era was revolutionary: Apparently immutable empires and monarchies, established for all eternity, were overthrown by communist and socialist revolutions. In 1917, Russia paved the way: Hungary and Germany soon followed. For most participants, it was a global movement in the making. Like his contemporaries, we must remember that Freud witnessed the social revolutions between the wars and generally approved of the movement—we will return to this. There are traces of Freud's theoretical political commitment until at least 1927; in his book, *The Future of an Illusion*, he justifies the rebellion of the masses against a culture in which a minority of individuals oppress the majority:

> If, however, a culture has not got beyond a point at which the satisfaction of one portion of its participants depends upon the suppression of another, and perhaps larger, portion—and this is the case in all present day cultures—it is understandable that the suppressed people should develop an intense hostility towards a culture whose existence they make possible by their work, but in whose wealth they have too small a share. In such conditions an internalization of the cultural prohibitions among the suppressed people is not to be expected … It goes without saying that a civilization which leaves so large a number of its participants unsatisfied and drives them into revolt neither has nor deserves the prospect of a lasting existence.[6]

This book is often understood in light of the anticommunism and anthropological pessimism of the next one, *Civilization and Its Discontents*. This position is justified politically by claiming that the masses are naturally unintelligent and inaccessible to arguments: Leaders are needed to make them obey. At the very least, this totally ignores the nuances of his position. In *Future*, Freud seriously considers the hypothesis that the oppressed people's failure in internalizing prohibitions is caused by the oppression by a minority. Indeed, in the same book, Freud limits his analysis and his critique to the cultural condition of "our own long-consolidated civilization."[7] In the introductory chapter, he takes care to distinguish this civilization from Russia's new revolutionary endeavor, about which he states he will suspend judgment. In this regard, psychoanalism undercuts Freud's ideas.[8] And more seriously, it disregards Freud's real practical orientation. Being strategically optimistic, Freud gave credence to progressive social reforms. Up until *The Future of an Illusion*, he recognized a minority's oppression and exploitation by the majority as a major cause of unhappiness in civilization that could be acted upon. It would then make sense for him to embrace projects like communism, which aim to improve people's material conditions. And so Freud directs the fire of his critique towards "our old civilization," to challenge the religious condition, which creates more disadvantages than advantages by keeping people ignorant and in an inhibition conducive to their domination (particularly women).

As opposed to popular belief, *The Future of an Illusion* should not only be understood in light of the discussion between Freud and his Swiss correspondent and friend, the pastor Oskar Pfister, a psychoanalyst who supported the combination of psychoanalysis and religion. At the very least, we must not remove this discussion from the revolutionary context Freud continuously references. Analyzing the future of the religious illusion took hold of Freud at this moment because it implicated the fate of society, as a whole as well as its transformations, particularly in terms of sexuality. This book is not only a general political reflection from an abstract metapsychological analytic point of view; it is also an analysis of the current situation that takes a political stance. The argument concerning the violence of the masses and the need to constrain them only makes sense within the hegemonic context of religious ideology, which Freud critiques, and which was, moreover, in decline. He sees an alternative: "Thus either these dangerous masses must be held down most severely and kept most carefully away from any chance of intellectual awakening, or else the relationship between civilization and religion must undergo a fundamental revision."[9] Of course, Freud advocates for the second solution, which he immediately compares to a "process of growth," similar to when a child becomes an adult. This is the reason, among others, that he sees religion as an infantile neurosis of humanity.[10] In recommending that this process be "encouraged," Freud moves from an evolutionist conception of societal progress to the political question of how this progress can be achieved in contemporary history. For him it consists in considering the "progress" of humans "reconciling" themselves with "their institutions"[11] and thus culture—not regarding culture's violence as an inevitable, ahistorical necessary evil. Of course, there are renunciations and privations necessary for the process of culture.[12] But not all of them are necessary. This is precisely the case of the "restrictions that apply only to certain classes of society," which Freud names the "underprivileged classes" (12).[13] By giving voice to an imaginary cynical and reactionary opponent (is it really Pfister, who complains in his correspondence with Freud about his conservative colleagues?), Freud presents his own historical and political perspective:

> Besides, have you learned nothing from history? Once before an attempt of this kind was made to substitute reason for religion, officially and in the grand manner. Surely you remember the French Revolution and Robespierre? And you must also remember how short-lived and miserably ineffectual the experiment was? The same experiment is being repeated in Russia at the present time![14]

Freud's position here in favor of revolution, in this case the Russian Revolution and its secular reforms, is largely ignored by the official field. But it is in fact widely known by experts in the history of psychoanalysis in Russia, who have long highlighted it.[15] Reich himself expressly points this out: "At any rate, Russia's initial social democracy was the most human approach possible under the existing historical conditions and given man's structure. Freud had explicitly admitted this."[16]

In the face of historical facts, we must remember that at the time Freud was not only not condemning Russian communism but, to a certain extent, defending it. Certainly without ignoring that things were going badly in the Russian Revolution, he explicitly declares that he does not have the "intention of making judgments," taking into account that this experiment was "unfinished"; he doesn't hesitate to describe it as a "great experiment in civilization" still underway, or to note "the grandeur of the plan and its importance for the future of human civilization."[17] Of course, he writes, "a certain percentage of humanity ... will always remain asocial" due to "an excess of instinctual strength."[18] However, an educational and cultural change should in fact be able to reduce the hostility of most of civilization. In this text, Freud defends *the possibility* of the communist hypothesis, insofar as it seems capable of achieving the reforms he calls for. Describing the human drives and the destructiveness of our "old civilization" does not prevent progressive change, nor does it exhaust the political possibilities—quite the contrary. Following his evolutionist and phylogenetic perspective, Freud indirectly argues for social progress that seems about to come true. Isn't the very aim of his book to envision a nonreligious education? This ambition is driven by a fully accepted hope of finding a "treasure to be dug up capable of enriching civilization": "By withdrawing their expectations from the other world and concentrating all their liberated energies into their life on earth, they will probably succeed in achieving a state of things in which life will become tolerable for everyone and civilization no longer oppressive to anyone."[19] It is therefore not surprising that a short time before—in 1926, according to Wilhelm Reich—Freud made remarks in a conversation that expressed "the hope that the revolutionary experiment in Soviet Russia would succeed."[20] Far from the pessimistic and supposedly apolitical context of the 1930s, to which we will return, we are interested first and foremost in this forgotten hope widely shared by all of the analysts in the 1920s.

Freud and Other Analysts' Commitment to Practice

The year 1917 was a veritable "dawning of the people," a clash of consciousnesses spread like wildfire across the world. The Russian Revolution offers hope of a better life for so many. It seems to herald a new era. Largely economically backward, Russia is propelled to the vanguard of the progressive politics being developed since the beginning of the century by various socialist and communist internationals. Gradually, the revolution expands and continues elsewhere ... The end of the Austro-Hungarian Empire takes place shortly after the Bolshevik revolution. Freud's city, Vienna, proclaims a republic, putting an end to six centuries of monarchy. Freud bears witness to the coming upheaval in his letters to Sándor Ferenczi, a psychoanalyst close to him: Despite the "muted tension" he feels, he cannot "suppress his satisfaction" at the idea of a "favorable outcome" that would see "a disintegration of the Prussian state."[21] In the same vein, just after armistice he writes: "The Hapsburgs left nothing on their way out except a load of crap."[22] Far from the orthodox reading that promotes the idea, based on a retrospective illusion, of an ideological split between the western European Freudian movement and revolutionary Russia,[23] the actors at the time understand this revolution as taking place within the same horizon as the political and ideological upheavals experienced by all of Europe.

During this intensely revolutionary moment, Freud gives his famous speech founding the policlinics in 1918:

And now in conclusion I will cast a glance at a situation which belongs to the future—one that will seem fantastic to many of you, but which I think, nevertheless, deserves that we should be prepared for it in our minds. You know that our therapeutic activities are not very far-reaching. There are only a handful of us, and even by working very hard each one can devote himself in a year to only a small number of patients. Compared to the vast amount of neurotic misery which there is in the world, and perhaps need not be, the quantity we can do away with is almost negligible. Besides this, the necessities of our existence limit our work to the well-to-do classes, who are accustomed to choose their own physicians and whose choice is diverted away from psycho-analysis by all kinds of prejudices ... At present we can do nothing for the wider social strata, who suffer extremely seriously from neuroses. Now let us assume that by some kind of organization we succeeded in increasing our numbers to an extent sufficient for treating a considerable mass of the population. On the other hand, it is possible to foresee that at some time or other the conscience of society will awake and remind it that the poor man should have just as much right to assistance for his mind as he now has to the life-saving help offered by surgery; and that the neuroses threaten public health no less than tuberculosis, and can be left as little as the latter to the impotent care of individual members of the community. When this happens, institutions or out-patient clinics will be started, to which analytically-trained physicians will be appointed, so that men who would otherwise give way to drink, women who have nearly succumbed under their burden of privations, children for whom there is no choice but between running wild or neurosis, may be made capable, by analysis, of resistance and of efficient work. Such treatments will be free.[24]

Given how essential this speech was for psychoanalysis, Freud's plea for a free psychoanalysis[25] throughout society was thus not a marginal issue. This is proved by the resounding success of this speech at the time, which allowed for the creation of more than a dozen policlinics in the biggest capitals. All the progressive actors were looking to the East, and many of them had been planning a future socialist society for a long time. The analysts' commitment to the policlinic project cannot be separated from this revolutionary horizon. Some even participated in it openly. Sándor Ferenczi—who at the time was convinced that psychoanalysts overlooked "the *real* conditions of different social classes" and abandoned the very people for whom daily life was particularly difficult[26]—was entrusted with the first chair of psychoanalysis in the Council of Republics in Hungary in the University of Budapest through the effort of the philosopher and revolutionary leader György Lukács.[27] He was also entrusted by a private clinic to open an analytic treatment center. Therefore, we must highlight that the first "institutionalization" of psychoanalysis took place in a revolutionary state.

With their positions on sexuality and education, analysts on the whole culturally complemented the political upheavals. A large majority of them were politically on the left. Ernst Simmel chaired the Society of Socialist Doctors. The more radical Helene Deutsch was close with Rosa Luxemburg. Freud himself was no exception.

In 1918, he placed his hopes on the figure of Victor Adler, the founder of the Second International bringing together the revolutionary Marxists and the reformist socialists,[28] and of whom Trotsky painted a glowing portrait.[29] Analysts promoted popular education, opened daycares, and struggled for the right to abortion. Freud supported the analytic attempts of his colleagues, such as Siegfried Bernfeld and August Aichhorn, who worked with juvenile delinquents. He helped found the magazine *Psychoanalytic Pedagogy*, in which all the major figures of psychoanalysis published.[30] In the middle of the 1920s, he gave his approval to the young analysts who decided to turn more towards the working class. Creating "outposts" that aimed to practice psychoanalysis in the very heart of working-class neighborhoods, these analysts went even further towards achieving Freud's wish of a people's psychoanalysis. With Erich Fromm and others, Karl Landauer established "the psychoanalytic worker community of Southeast Germany,"[31] and Reich, along with four other analysts and three obstetricians, opened six centers for sexual hygiene, "immediately full to bursting,"[32] in order to spread information about child education and contraception to the working class.

Freud often ranted about Vienna and its bourgeois authorities, especially when he and his colleagues were prevented from opening a policlinic in the city for a few years. At the same time, he was well known and recognized in a city that was conducting radical social projects, and he even signed up for one of the Social Democratic Worker's Party's campaigns of distributing baby clothes to unemployed families. The famous anatomist and brilliantly accomplished academic Julius Tandler, who, as administrator of the new republic's welfare system, did much to lower the infant mortality rate, acknowledges this: "there was little controversy about Freud's role in Vienna," adding that he was "without a doubt one of the most influential men of the era."[33] Named a citizen of honor, Freud donated part of the money raised for his seventieth birthday to the policlinic, which had finally opened. Like other Viennese doctors in the 1920s, Freud wrote up *Erlagscheine* for his treatment sessions, vouchers that acted as an alternative currency which could be redeemed in cash or in time, a typical innovation from Red Vienna.[34] In a letter to Paul Federn, a member of the psychoanalytic society and the city municipal council, Freud asserted that "being poor is no longer a disgrace today."[35] The practice and debates that inspired the analysts at the time focused on "unconventional methods." They argued for "gender equality," "decriminalization of homosexuality," and "sexual liberation."[36]

At the time, psychoanalysis contributed to, and even preceded, politics, with its new practice showing the way forward. In his Budapest speech, Freud makes clear what is at stake in the relationship of the state with the policlinics: They are set up *with the expectation* that the state "comes to see these duties as urgent" and takes them up since at "some time or other ... it must come to this."[37] Generally speaking, we must admit that the political context lent itself favorably to this view. The old world and its traditions were crumbling and psychoanalysis seemed to be opening new horizons that would be crucial. Influenced by the text *Psychoanalysis of the Masses* by the founder of the Berlin policlinic, Ernst Simmel, the German government came close to creating a chair of psychoanalysis.[38] As we have seen, this would become a reality in the Hungarian revolution of 1919, where Ferenczi attests: "Psychoanalysis is being courted from all sides, I find it hard to turn down every advance."[39] But in the end, the experiment went furthest in Russia, where a State Psychoanalytic Institute was established, including clinics and a home for children. Freud's wish for a free community-supported people's psychotherapy—a wish that had otherwise united all of the leading figures of psychoanalysis in creating private policlinics—was being achieved in the land of the Soviets. "Impressed" by the Russian undertaking, Freud, along with Anna Freud and Marie Bonaparte, gave his support. Apart from Jones (who incidentally had not attended the founding Budapest Congress), most analysts sang the praises of the Children's Home.[40] "Perhaps the light comes from the east,"[41] Freud confided to Reich. For most analysis in those revolutionary years, the Russian experiment undeniably represented hope for the progressive movements in Europe, in which they actively participated.

The Sexual Revolution and Psychoanalysis in the Russian Revolution

Psychoanalysis was well known in Russia before 1917, particularly among the intellectual elite. A significant number of the revolution's architects were supportive of it, since for them it was a question of changing lives, a daunting task in the Russian context. Before the revolution, family laws were contained in the "Svod Zakonov," or the compendium of laws of the Russian Empire, which among other things allowed parents to imprison their disobedient children. Marriage was a sacrament; divorce did not exist; the Orthodox Church and its moralism exerted a massive hold on individual psychic life. Psychoanalysis would make it possible to rethink areas such as education, relationships between men and women, the family, and sexuality on a nonreligious basis. This is why, once the revolutionaries came to power they made room for it in the construction of the new social regime.

But interest in psychoanalysis went far beyond the new authorities' circle. There was a real fad for psychoanalysis among the revolutionary Russian youth in the 1920s. Pamphlets on Freud and the sexual revolution from the German revolutionary circles, particularly feminist ones, circulated widely—to the extent that Lenin, opposed to this approach, denounced it as counter-revolutionary. Clara Zetkin, a feminist figure in the German Communist Party close to Lenin, was astounded to hear him declare:

> I have been told that at the evenings arranged for reading and discussion with working women, sex and marriage problems come first. They are said to be the main objects of interest in your political instruction and educational work ... It is said that a pamphlet on the sex question written by a Communist authoress from Vienna enjoys the greatest popularity. What rot that booklet is! ... The mention of Freud's hypotheses is designed to give the pamphlet a scientific veneer, but it is so much bungling by an amateur.[42]

Despite this hostility, under the impetus of feminism the Russian Revolution would go on to assert women's rights more than any other regime of the time. Alexandra Kollontaï, one of the first women ambassadors in 1923, created the Jenotdel with Inès Armand, a department responsible for women's issues close to the Central Committee. All the backward values underlying the education and family system of the previous society were challenged. They promoted new forms of romantic relationships and passed sexual reform laws. "Youth communes," part of the Komsomols,[43] tried to break free from family life by practicing free love in an autonomous and collectivist manner. Some factions of the official revolutionary movement to the left of Lenin and Trotsky openly accepted the promotion of other bonds of love than the family.[44] For this liberatory[45] current (very popular then), the abolition of the division of labor and its inequalities went along with the abolition of what we would call today "gender inequality," in an attempt to enact sexual liberation perfectly.[46] Alongside the eight-hour work day and land rights, the right to vote was given to women, equal pay for equal skills was passed, and maternity leave was implemented. Shortly after October, civil marriage and the freedom of divorce was instituted. The decree of January 23, 1918, proclaimed the complete separation of church and state. From then on, love life and its ties, as well as children's schooling, were liberated from the old shackles. The 1919 party platform went even further and arranged for the socialization of domestic work in order to liberate women. Plans for public dining halls, nurseries, and kindergartens were created. The new laws also allowed spouses to choose their last name: the woman's or man's or both.[47] Adultery and homosexuality were removed from the penal code, and the authority of the head of the family was removed from the civil code. And finally, in 1920, abortion was legalized—the first government in Europe to legalize abortion.[48] The sexual reform introduced by the revolutionaries became a "model" for many reformers and intellectuals around the world.[49] The most daring and avant-garde experiments took place in Russia, often beyond the reach of any centralizing organization.[50] How could psychoanalysis, this new science of sex and the unconscious, not have a legitimate place in this context? Its breakthrough in Russia followed the revolutionary momentum, and many of Russia's top leaders were sympathetic to it.

An analyst well known before the war[51] and politically engaged since the first Russian Revolution of 1905, Tatiana Rosenthal continued after 1917 to care for mentally ill patients using psychoanalysis, while also directing a school for street kids in the revolutionary city of Petrograd. In her eyes, there was no disconnect between Marx and Freud—in fact, it was a conviction held by many analysts of the era.[52] With this in mind, the State Psychoanalytic Institute was created a few years after the revolution. Martin Pappenheim, a member of the Vienna Psychoanalytic Society close to Freud, claimed after returning from a trip to Russia that "in Moscow, there is considerable interest in psychoanalysis." Some Russian analysts' texts had already been published in "Freud's journal."[53] Psychoanalysis was officially taught in institutions like any other discipline. The Soviet government publishing house (Gosizdat) formed "The New Russian Psychoanalytic Bookshop." The collection was a success—the stock of psychoanalytic texts was quickly depleted and constantly reprinted. Better still, many psychiatric clinics and shelters treated patients for free using psychoanalytic methods. Freud's wish in his Budapest speech came true: The poor had a right to psychoanalysis just as they had a right to surgery. It therefore made sense that Freud, like the vast majority of his colleagues, supported the Russian Bolshevik analysts and the Russian Society of Psychoanalysis joining the International Psychoanalytic Association (IPA).[54]

The Psychoanalysis of Children and Education in Revolutionary Russia

In 1921, Melanie Klein formulated expectations that, at the time, seemed to be far in the future:

> How can upbringing on psycho-analytic principles be carried out in practice? The requirement so firmly established by analytic experience that parents, nurses and teachers should themselves be analysed will probably remain a pious wish for a long time yet. [...] I would here like to make a suggestion that is only a counsel of necessity but that transitionally might be efficacious until other times bring other possibilities. I mean the founding of Kindergartens at the head of which there will be women analysts. There is no doubt that a woman analyst who has under her a few nurses trained by her can observe a whole crowd of children so as to recognize the suitability of analytic intervention and to carry it out forthwith.[55]

However, when Vera Schmidt and her husband went to Berlin and Vienna in October 1923 to report on the Russian psychoanalytic movement, Melanie Klein's wish had already come true. Vera Schmidt was a founding member of the Russian Society of Psychoanalysis and a practicing analyst. Trained in the pedagogical methods of the kindergarten founder Friedrich Fröbel, who championed a pedagogy based on the importance of play for toddlers, Schmidt worked in the Children's Department in the Commissariat of Public Education. In this context, she created an experimental children's home that included toddlers, the Destike Dom [Children's Home].[56]

In analytic circles, where conventional approaches were being challenged, pedagogy had long been a key area of study. In 1908, Ferenczi wrote in *Psychoanalysis and Education*:

> present-day education is literally a forcing house for various neuroses. [...] even an education inspired by the noblest intentions and carried out under the most favourable conditions has, through being based on faulty but generally accepted principles now prevalent, a harmful influence in many respects upon the development of the child [...] we learn that even he who by good luck has not become ill has, nevertheless, endured much unnecessary mental pain and suffering because of inappropriate pedagogical methods and theories.[57]

In short, it was a matter of not leaving education to licensed teachers. The postwar political climate at last seemed conducive to other approaches. Psychoanalytically oriented educational experiments had already been tried in the West, particularly in Berlin in 1919 with the Kinderheim Baumgarten, a home school for homeless children under Bernfeld's care. It was also the period when analysis of children was being developed by Hermine Hug-Hellmuth, Berta Bornstein, Melanie Klein, and Anna Freud. If these approaches began to influence existing institutions, the Russian experiment of the Home, where they explicitly promoted "an education based on analytic principles," was the vanguard.

The issue of progressive education had been set as an absolute priority of the new socialist state. For Lenin, education had been turned into "a blockade impeding workers' children from advancing" and this blockade

Figure 1 Vera Schmidt

must "be torn down."[58] Pre-revolutionary Russia was still a backwards country with an enormous cultural lag: More than three-quarters of the population was illiterate and 80 percent of children did not go to school. But the revolutionaries understood education as a key to forming a socialist society.

Practice in the Children's Home

Claiming psychoanalysis's superiority over classic pedagogy was nothing trivial: It involved a complete reversal of the order that had hitherto dictated educational practices. The child or toddler was not only recognized as a person in their own right—which was already in itself a true revolution when recalling the "Zvod Zakonov" (The Digest of the Laws [of the Russian Empire])—they were also viewed through the manifestations of their polymorphous sexuality and in their appetite for knowledge, two key aspects specifically denied to them by classic pedagogy. Early on, Freud questioned pedagogy and its true goals: "To be sure, if it is the purpose of educators to stifle the child's power of independent thought as early as possible, in favour of the 'goodness' which they think so much of, they cannot set about this better than by deceiving him in sexual matters and intimidating him in matters of religion."[59] Indeed Freud had shown the structural link between sexual repression and the decline of scientific curiosity, which together result in the "fear of thinking." Thus, against classical education, Vera Schmidt attached great importance to the infantile desire for knowledge and the adult's truthful relationship with the child in their quest for knowledge.[60]

Melanie Klein also insisted on this point. Censorship and lies are disastrous for the "child's instinct for knowledge": "If natural curiosity and the impulse to enquire into unknown as well as previously surmised facts and phenomena is opposed, then the more profound enquiries [...] are also repressed along with it. Simultaneously, however, all impulses to investigate deeper questions in general become also inhibited."[61] Like her Western counterparts, Schmidt recommended openness and sincerity, which is put into practice in the responses given to children in the home, trusting the child and their intellectual abilities. Thanks to a language within their grasp, children become reachable through scientific realism, which deep down they are waiting for. It is also a way to prepare the child for reality while protecting them from religious illusions. But such a radically new approach entails a revolution in practice, first and foremost on the part of the educator.

When the child is not repressed in their desire for knowledge but instead accompanied, the educator can then begin "serious work"—an analysis—in order to "free themselves from the prejudices that their own education bequeathed them." The child's healthy development depends "on their relationship with the educator."[62] This wager on the role of transference in the pedagogical relationship leads to a number of changes in the relationship between educator and child. By successive strokes, Schmidt subtly deconstructs the authoritarianism that presided over the old education:

> Renouncing the satisfaction of the drives should not be achieved through a prohibition pronounced by the

teacher. The child should not stop soiling themselves just because they must not soil themselves, but because they slowly learn that they can also remain clean.[63]

Instead of giving direct orders to the child, which will only bring about their resistance, we should explain rationally, even at the youngest age, what we expect of them.[64]

The educator trained in analysis becomes sensitive to the question of the child's psychosexual development, which is the focus of their pedagogical attention. This is how the teacher favors the pathways of sublimation by proposing, for example, appropriate games (sand, drawing, etc.) for the different identified stages (oral, anal, etc.). Likewise, they respond honestly to the questions the child asks. This reversal of practices, which signals the recognition of the child as a subject, is only possible because "the authority of the teacher is replaced by contact with the child through transference." In this way, the law imposed on the child is slowly introjected through the relationship with the educator, rather than suffered or arbitrarily imposed from the outside. Psychoanalysis becomes the prerequisite for any real pedagogical work. Schmidt does not compromise on this point: If "despite their efforts" and "their personal analysis," a teacher "is unable to regard infantile sexual manifestations without repulsion or disgust, then they would be better off giving up the role of teacher altogether."[65]

For Vera Schmidt, the analysis imperative for pedagogues to overcome their own prejudices also meets a need on a completely different scale. It is a matter of curbing a deadly and unnecessary repetition instructed by culture, and of which the teacher is only a cog. In *The Future of an Illusion*, Freud claims that if humans are "so entirely governed by their instinctual wishes" and "so little accessible to reasonable arguments," it is not because their "innermost nature necessitates it." It is not an "anthropological" cause that prevents the subject's access to thought but instead religious education.[66] In support of this social approach to the subject, and contrary to a widespread constitutionalist approach that consisted in naturalizing the characteristics of subjects and peoples, Freud asks:

> Can an anthropologist give the cranial index of a people whose custom it is to deform their children's heads by bandaging them round from their earliest years? Think of the depressing contrast between the radiant intelligence of a healthy child and the feeble intellectual powers of the average adult. Can we be quite certain that it is not precisely religious education which bears a large share of the blame for this relative atrophy?[67]

But, from the beginning of the twentieth century, the Freudian clinical approach responded to this critical interrogation into sociopolitical causality. Freud asks, "What can be the purpose of withholding from children—or, let us say, from young people—enlightenment of this kind about the sexual life of human beings [...] Is it from a hope that a concealment of this kind may retard the sexual instinct altogether until such time as it can find its way into the only channels open to it in our middle-class [bourgeois] social order?"[68] Freud was thus calling for this reform all the while knowing "the impossibility of carrying out an isolated reform without altering the foundations of the whole system"[69] in countries where religion had a stranglehold on education, as was the case with Russia. This was precisely Schmidt's perspective. In fact, long after the home closed in 1924 and Stalin took control of power, Freud continued to assert these civilizational needs: He speaks of a "treasure to be dug up" and "a hope for the future"[70] generated by the prospect of a psychoanalytically oriented education.

2
Wilhelm Reich: From the Vienna Policlinic to the Sexpol in Berlin

When Wilhelm Reich arrived in Vienna in 1918, he was not driven by revolutionary ideals but by necessity. An orphan at fourteen, he came from a Ukrainian peasant family that lost everything during the war. Alone, penniless, and clueless, the young Reich came to Vienna to pursue his studies. He would choose medicine and psychiatry.[1] The city was at that time an epicenter for cultural and political movements. Fauvism, atonal music, futurism, and movements for the emancipation of women, as well as psychoanalysis and learned epistemological debates about science, were already "at work" in the Weimar Republic since before the war; but in the beginning of the 1920s, the city that Reich was discovering was at its boiling point. If, like all the other analysts of his generation, he was carried away by this atmosphere, his political consciousness took shape gradually: It would emerge from the very heart of his practice in the Vienna policlinic.

The Clinical Foundations of Reich's Political Commitment: The Policlinic

Reich thus embarked on his studies in medicine and psychiatry. In particular, he took courses with the eminent

Dr. Tandler, reformer of the welfare system mentioned earlier. During his training, he took part in a seminar on sexology. He gave a paper on "The Concepts of Instinct and Libido from Forel to Jung," in which Freud's concepts were given pride of place. He claims that the discovery of Freud's theories was a "relief" for him, especially *Three Essays on Sexuality*, which revolutionized previous concepts. Sexuality did not appear at puberty, there was an infantile sexuality: "Freud had paved a road to a clinical understanding of sexuality. He showed that adult sexuality proceeds from stages of sexual development in childhood."[2] Reich met the Viennese master, who made a deep impression on him. But he was most struck by his clinical concern: "I was deeply moved by the earnestness with which Freud sought to comprehend mental patients. His views were head and shoulders above the 'priggishly conceited' opinions which the psychiatrists of the old school expressed about mental illness. As they saw it, some things were simply 'crazy.'"[3] As opposed to the many analyses that affirm Freud's lack of interest in the clinic, the young Reich's meeting with Freud was sealed around a common interest in patients. From then on, Reich quickly played an important role in psychoanalysis. In 1920, when he was barely 22, he become a member of the Psychoanalytic Society of Vienna and was quickly offered a position of responsibility. When the Vienna policlinic was founded in 1922, he was named the first assistant alongside Hitschmann and Freud. He became the vice-director from 1928 to 1930.

Immersed in the clinic, Reich found himself confronted with his patients' distress. This is the reason that, from the outset, the question of analytic technique and also of the scope of treatment played such a decisive role in his activity as well as his publications: It was a matter of knowing how to care for people. From 1924 to 1930, he held a seminar at the policlinic on analytic technique, in which he discussed concrete cases and tried to explain the positive outcomes of treatment as well as the impasses faced by the practitioner. At the time, analysts liked to think that a treatment could lead to a recovery in just a few months. Reich found that the reality was quite different, and that the analyst comes up against innumerable obstacles. When he opened up to Freud, he responded: "Above all ... analysis means patience. The unconscious is timeless."[4] But this theoretical response did not satisfy him: "Freud was a master in theoretically unraveling the intricacies of a complicated situation. But, regarding technique, his explanations were unsatisfying."[5] Freud took six years to analyze the Wolf-Man; but the patients Reich saw were too poor to carry out such lengthy work, and the institution where Reich practiced—which struggled to meet all the demand—certainly didn't allow it. Even if all the analysts in the policlinic were to provide a free hour of analysis for patients, this was far from sufficient to keep up with the crowds. How could they deal with the urgency of these situations and the patients' distress, all of which were very real and deserved therapy? Freud, however, pointed to a way: It was necessary to "analyze the resistances." Reich explored this path in depth until he formulated new theoretical proposals on "character analysis," which would allow him to solve the problems encountered in treatment, and which Freud would support without reservations.⁶

Reich's Seminar at the Policlinic

While the founder of psychoanalysis gave backing to Reich's seminar (right to the end), it was not the same for his older colleagues. They did not like Reich's approach to the problems of psychoanalytic practice: "anyone who wants to bring clarity to the controversial question of analytic therapy and refuses to become stifled in his interest in psychoanalysis as a science and movement is looked upon with a jaundiced eye ... Whence stems this shyness to discuss our therapy?"⁷ For him, it was actually a symptom. While his well-established colleagues only shared successful treatments or simply scorned the subject—adopting the prejudice based on the idea that Freud did not have a high opinion of therapeutics—Reich spoke about his failures and tried to explain them in public discussions. This attitude certainly got him into trouble with his elders in the IPA, but it brought him great success with the young generation of analysts who came to listen to him. This is the case, for example, with Richard Sterba, who gives us this invaluable commentary:

> [Reich] had an unusual flair for psychic dynamics. His clinical astuteness and his technical skill made him an excellent teacher and his technical seminar was so instructive that many of the older members of the society attended it regularly [...] Reich was particularly brilliant in his synopsis of the report, which he

organized according to his excellent understanding of the dynamics of the presented material. His technical advice to the person who reported gave me the basic understanding of the handling of the transference and of resistances.[8]

His investigations and the questions that he gave free rein to in his seminar, as well as his success with young people in training and the protection Freud gave him, aroused jealousy and made the more experienced analysts uneasy—all the more so as Reich conducted research in the name of clinical objectives that were difficult to contest.[9] Paul Federn, a friend of Freud from the first generation of psychoanalysts, even tried to remove him from leading his own seminar, but Freud opposed it.[10] For his part, Reich had avoided making presentations to the IPA since 1923, when he gave his talk on "On 'Genitality' from the Standpoint of Psychoanalytic Prognosis and Therapy." In this paper, based on 28 cases of male neu-

Figure 2 Wilhelm Reich, circa 1943

rosis and 14 of female neurosis, he already set out to give an account of processes unexplained by classical theory. It was on this occasion that he put forward his ideas on the genital primacy, insisting on the importance of resolving the current neurosis.[11] Rereading this paper today, Reich's great mastery of the articulation of the clinical with the theoretical, which he discusses in an original way, seems evident.[12] He does not just act as an epistemologist or a theoretician, but also a therapist who cares about his patients.

In the 1922 congress in Berlin, Freud suggested the question of mutual relation between theory and therapy as a subject for an essay prize. Reich didn't show up and no competitor took the prize. But there is no doubt that Reich's paper in 1923, like his further developments, were a continuation of Freud's call to conduct such an investigation.

Confronted with his patients and with clinical necessity, Reich endeavored, following Freud's indications, to focus the analysis "on the resistances" in order to remove them. In three of his patients, however, he noted that the breakdown of their resistances through analysis was accompanied by a lifting of repression and healing. The lifting of repression allowed the libido that had been frozen to discharge itself sexually: There was a recovery of the function of the orgasm. Without going through the time-consuming and expensive uncovering of the unconscious in search of infantile causes—a search that does not always lead to a favorable outcome—the clinic showed that there is a much faster therapeutic possibility through the genital libido. To account for these observations theoretically, Reich took up Freud's idea of a current neurosis, which he had never abandoned. As opposed to the classic psychoneurosis, the current neurosis was in theory not analyzable because its source was in a recent disturbance. It was the immediate result of repressed sexuality and thus did not have a psychic etiology. This is why, according to Freud, a simple treatment could be applied: It was enough to eliminate the "harmful"[13] sexual practices for neurosis to disappear. But Freud had never ruled out that perhaps at the heart of all psychoneurosis was a current neurosis, that is, a current sexual problem in which it found its energy. Moreover, Reich argued, analysis could reveal as well that every current neurosis also had a psychoneurosis for its superstructure, that is, an infantile psychic conflict. The general idea of Reich's study was to unify the theory of neuroses, and to show the decisive place of the economic aspect of the neurosis in the handling of transference and treatment.[14] Although these views were well founded and well argued—and did not conflict with Freud's perspective but even extended them—they were received by the official members of the association with an "arctic chill," according to Reich himself.

Reich trained new analysts awaiting his help and interventions, with whom he enjoyed a large audience. Practically all of the third-generation analysts attended his seminar, including Anna Freud, the master's daughter. These young analysts who were just starting and did not have private clients were faced with the same problems and questions that Reich had in his daily practice with patients in the policlinic. Though he preferred to conduct his investigations within the framework of the seminar, the freedom he gained there was difficult for the old generation to bear.

This generational conflict was also echoed at the Berlin policlinic around another important figure in the politically committed psychoanalytic movement, Otto Fenichel. Outside the policlinic, he set up a seminar called, "Children's Seminar," which brought together young analysts. But while this seminar in Berlin was based on an explicit political disagreement,[15] Reich's seminar was so successful—and the target of attacks—for reasons related to psychoanalysis, his clinic, and his technique. Perhaps we have not made sufficient note that Reich's sociopolitical consciousness emerged precisely from this crucible of clinic and technical reflection. In other words, and not without paradox, Reich's political commitment—for which he was so criticized and later expelled from the IPA—was forged from the first years of his practice in the very heart of the Viennese analytic movement's orthodoxy and in the daily practice of the policlinic.

The Poor Patients of the Vienna Policlinic

In the policlinic, Reich took in "all-comers" in accordance with its founding objective. Yet the distress felt by his patients was intimately linked to their appalling social deprivation. As opposed to the Berlin policlinic, where, as its president and principal funder, Max Eitingon, highlighted, "the authentically proletarian elements have disappeared," in Vienna, patients were all from the working class. Reich states: "There were industrial workers, office clerks, students, and farmers from the country. The influx was so great that we were at a loss to deal with it."[16] Reich would gradually devote most of his research and clinical time to them. His practice "brought [him] a wealth of insights and observations about the neuroses of the economically low," which also made up the subject of his first book, *The Impulsive Character* (1925). There, Reich describes people bearing the brunt of economic poverty, who were at risk of falling into crime: "As a result of material distress, the moralistic inhibitions had been broken down to such an extent that the criminal and perverse impulses clamored for action."[17] Against the science of his time, Reich would show that patients labeled by psychiatry as "psychopaths" or "antisocial degenerates," victims of "moral madness" for which heredity was the sole cause, actually had social and psychological reasons for being what they were. A few years before, Reich wrote a first monograph on his "difficult" patients, which the private practice ignored. From the metapsychological point of view, the lack of inhibitions from which they suffered reflected a particular situation of their ego in relation to the agency supposed to regulate it, the superego. He submitted this monograph to Freud, who wrote him a letter of wholehearted support. According to Freud, Reich's case studies, in which what seemed like "defects" in the structure of the ego manifested themselves, could only be of great interest for psychoanalytic research. It was possible that "from now on mechanisms similar to those which had been found to be operative between ego and id would be found to be operative between ego and superego."[18]

Reich specifically went on to detail and clarify these mechanisms. The formation of the ego ideal and the possibility of ambivalence for the subject depends on the satisfaction of the drives, conditioned by the attitude of the educator that they had known as a child. Reich's patients, however, came from poor backgrounds, and experienced very troubled childhoods and "education." Exposed to poverty and overcrowding, they grew up as well as they could. Left to themselves, often too early victims of sexual transgression by an adult, the children they had been were not aware of the benefit of the prohibition that should have protected them from abuse. However, the prohibition would sooner or later be found in the form of social or even legal repression (at this time, vagrancy, for example, was punished by the law). It would then manifest in a brutal way: Children or adolescents would come up against it violently, without understanding it. How could they accept it and integrate the law? In other words, impulsive character formation depended on a particular educational environment:

> Clearly, an environment marked by scanty impulse control makes for poor ego ideal formation in the child; on the other hand, it allows the impulse frustration to be more brutal than necessary. Hence the typically acute and outspoken ambivalence of the impulsive, who can rightly say that he was not taught any differently.[19]

For Reich, the psychic distress affecting these patients was thus inextricably linked to their poverty-stricken social condition, so that one and the other tended to merge. On the one hand, his patients' psychic structure, formed by harsh social constraints they experienced in childhood, was such that it constantly led them to make impulsive decisions; at the same time, on the other hand, their miserable social condition as adults was struck by the same repression they experienced as children and condemned them to such choices. This condition confined them, it was what indeed they had always known, what was most familiar to them. It had encouraged traumatic elements in childhood and contributed to their repetition. The circle was complete—a vicious circle.

Reich's thesis revealed several crucial points for psychoanalytic discipline, as well as for psychiatry. Not only did the argument that analysis was impossible for these cases that had been wrongly labeled "narcissistic" collapse but it also became clear that the clinic was inextricably linked with political and social issues. For Reich, however,

> Neither the psychiatrist nor the psychoanalyst thought to inquire into the social living conditions of the patients. It was known, of course, that there was poverty and material distress, but somehow this was not regarded as being relevant to the treatment. Yet, the patient's material conditions were a constant problem in the clinic.[20]

Reich would argue for the recognition of the pre-eminent role of material and social conditions in his poor patients' discomfort. Impulsive character disorders were first and foremost due to their past and current social condition. From this stemmed the "impossible life" of those who were called "marginal" or whose behavior psychiatry characterized as "moral insanity."[21]

Reich's Fragment of an Analysis of a Working Woman

Reading one of Reich's fragments of analysis gives us a concrete view of the ideas he was putting forward. This case is one of the most serious and moving cases he was dealing with on a daily basis. It shows the difficulties he faced and the solutions he invented to overcome the classic conception of theory and technique he had inherited:

> One day, a pretty young working woman came to the clinic. She had two boys and a small child with her. She had lost her voice, a symptom known as "hysterical mutism." She wrote on a slip of paper that she had suddenly lost her voice a few days before. Since an analysis was not possible, I made an attempt to eliminate the speech disturbance through hypnosis and was successful after a few sessions. Now she spoke in a low, hoarse, and apprehensive voice. For years she had been suffering from a compulsive impulse to kill her children. The father of the children had deserted her. She was alone, and she and the children had hardly anything to eat. She did sewing at home, but earned hopelessly little from it. Then she was struck by the idea of murder. She was on the verge of pushing her children into the water when she was seized by terrible anxiety. From then on she was tormented by the impulse to confess to the police to protect the children from herself. This intention put her in a state of deadly fear. She was afraid of being hanged for her crime. The thought of it produced a constriction in her throat. The mutism protected herself against carrying out her impulse.[22]

This case—where current social deprivation is inextricably linked to psychical symptoms—speaks for itself. But there is more. In fact, exploring the infantile history of the patient also showed the effects of social deprivation on her psychic suffering: The current symptom of constriction of the throat bore the unconscious trace of this suffering. She was orphaned early and raised by strangers. With six or more people living in a single room, Reich explains, she had to endure the sexual assault of adults. Since childhood, the burning desire for a protective mother tormented her, which was reflected in her fantasies where she saw herself become a safe baby, sucking her mother's breast. But now that she was a mother, she realized that she was seeing her children in a similar situation to the one she had experienced as a child. She was unable to feed them, which was unbearable. Her symptom of constriction of the throat was not only due to her current fear of police repression but also tied to the whole tragic history of the patient, the early loss of her mother, the resulting exposure to danger, and the miserable social conditions and overcrowding she lived through. All this made her desire the figure of a mother who would have been able to protect her and feed her, to the point of conceiving this regressive, reparative fantasy. The current neurosis's symptom of constriction derived its energy from the patient's condition of social deprivation, where she faced the inability to feed her children. Her fear of the police and punishment fit in well with an older psychoneurotic infantile history, which was susceptible to analysis. As Reich said in a clear clinical formula: "Throat and neck had always been the site of the choking anxiety and the longing."[23] But this psychoneurosis was itself related to the extreme social deprivation the young woman had grown up in, and its specificity made it that much less accessible to analysis since everything in the patient's current condition was competing to repeat these psychic and material details tragically. Reich visited his patient many times in the Vienna slums and stated:

> There was nothing, absolutely nothing, to bring light into this life. There was nothing but misery, loneliness, gossip of the neighbors, worries about the next meal—and, on top of it all, there were the criminal chicaneries of her landlord and employer. In spite of the fact that she was severely hampered in her work by acute psychic disturbances, she was ruthlessly exploited. She received some two schillings per day for ten hours' work. That is to say, she was expected to support herself and her three children on some sixty to eighty schillings per month! The phenomenal thing about it was: she did it! I was never able to find out how she managed.[24]

Taking Social Deprivation into Account in the Determination of Neuroses and Their New Therapeutic Needs

Poor and isolated mothers, young girls subject to sexual assault due to overcrowded living spaces, unemployed workers on the brink of suicide—how can the influence of social condition on neurosis be ignored? How can its impact on psychic life not be taken into consideration? Reich was upset. He raged against his colleagues' blindness, bad faith, and misguidance: Should we really search for the cause of a couple's sexual inhibitions in their infantile experiences when we know that they live in only one room with several children? This is how he developed his reflections on class differences in the expression of neurosis. While among the affluent, symptoms related to "obsessional behaviors," "hysterical twilight states," "fantasies of murder," or even "murderous impulses," seem relatively harmless, among poor patients they take on a "dangerous character."[25] Social constraint has effects on two levels. On the one hand, the deprivation and economic necessity in which the subject finds itself weakens the superego and its inhibitions, exposing it to the greatest dangers. On the other hand, "working-class neuroses" do not have the cultural material that allows them to follow the path of sublimation. For these reasons, the subject's psychic misery and material misery tend to merge: "The neuroses of the working population are merely lacking in cultural finesse ... the well-to-do citizen bears his neurosis with dignity, or he manifests it materially in one form or another. Among the broad masses of the working population, the neurosis comes out in all its tragic grotesqueness."[26]

Soon the difference between private clients and hospital clients became "obvious and fundamental" to Reich: "After we had been working for two years or so, it became clear that individual psychotherapy has a very limited significance."[27] But if the classic technique of archaeological investigation, which assumes a long analysis time, did not lend itself to the cases studied by Reich, it is not because of "psychiatric disorder" or a "constitutional defect in intelligence." These subjects did not present evidence of a different psychical nature than that of the "neurotics," but, more simply, of totally degraded social conditions. If the technique failed, we should not blame the subject but rather the therapist who purports to use it on a subject they know nothing about. The fact that it does not "work" does not reveal the "hereditary taint" of an "unanalyzable" subject but the social discoordination [dysmétrie sociale] working-class subjects experience in relation to subjects from the wealthier classes. The working-class subject is plunged into an infinitely greater psychic emergency and social constraint, forcing the analyst to find new paths. The pain these neurotics experience requires taking things in reverse. This is why, from a theoretical point of view, Reich insists on his idea of current neurosis and its treatment. For the analyst, a new clinical approach to intervention emerges because it is the social conditions of the most deprived that currently make them sick. Therefore, the neurosis is current in the sense that it tends to merge with the patient's present psychic and social situation, just as, if the analysis is able to go further, this situation would reveal itself to be closely linked with their infantile history. In concrete terms, by tackling certain aspects of social deprivation like abortion, crime, contraception, or education, but also by interpreting them from the point of view of sexual dynamics, the analyst could act upon the neuroses. To that end, it was necessary to intervene more in society, which led Reich in 1929 to create six sexual hygiene centers, in addition to the policlinic.

Even though Freud did not agree with the latest developments in Reich's theory (on genitality, the function of the orgasm, etc.), he approved of his direction. But was it even something new? Wasn't this simply a further development of Freud's project for the prevention of neurosis, which was at the very origin of the founding of the policlinics? Freud's support for Reich's work suggests that. Besides, at the time, Freud had not yet formulated his pessimistic theory of civilization, which tended to essentialize aggression in the individual and to present civilization and its repression as a necessary evil. On the contrary, as we have seen, in 1927 he recognized the repression suffered by the masses and the likely cultural benefit from acting on it. At that time, Freud clearly stated that some of the deprivations imposed on those "left behind" were not at all necessary for civilization. Rather, these deprivations jeopardize it and undermine its legitimacy. From this point of view, the preventative dimension, as specified by Reich and to which he was committed until the creation of the sexual hygiene centers in 1929, could certainly contribute to civilization and was perfectly in line with Freud's vision.

Prevention of Neurosis and Communist Militancy

It wasn't just the individual clinical problems associated with the social deprivation he encountered at the policlinic that launched Reich into this new and highly instructive course of action. It was also the events related to the riots in Vienna on July 15 and 16, 1927. These two days, which left a vivid impression on him, pushed him towards a commitment to militancy and opened up new analytic questions.

On January 30, monarchist war veterans shot into the crowd at a social democratic rally, killing two and wounding two more. But when the killers were acquitted in court on July 14, a strike was called for the morning of the 15th. Workers occupied Vienna's center, setting fire to the courthouse. The police were firing at point-blank throughout the city: By the morning, there were more than 100 dead. Reich, who participated in the demonstration, hid with his wife in a park. Shocked by the situation, he saw it as the defeat of social democracy. It was a political turning point for him: That same evening he joined a communist organization, the Workers' [International] Relief, a kind of Red Cross for the party.

This event also allowed him to verify the accuracy in the field of the theories on recruitment and identification with the leader Freud proposed in his 1921 book *Group Psychology and Analysis of the Ego*. The police's behavior was mechanical and disaffected. They blindly obeyed orders to shoot. However, Reich was surprised to see the crowd let itself be massacred by police forces when it was large enough to tear them to shreds. What held the protestors back from attacking the police, when it was in their interest to do so? What allowed the crowd to tolerate hours of sporadic gunfire? This questioning led to a new heuristic, enabling him to elaborate the social function of sexual repression.

In this period, Reich also began to read Marx and Engels, whose theories he drew on in his thinking. At the same time, he discovered the "classics" of modern sociology and anthropology on which Marx and Engels based their work: The Swiss sociologist Johann Jakob Bachofen, who had studied matriarchy, and Lewis Henry Morgan, who was the first to look at kinship systems. As Reich attests, these were crucial readings, not only for his political education but also for his psychoanalytic approach to anthropology.[28] But, above all, it was his encounter with the workers and the proletariat in the Red slums and the therapeutic action conducted among them that helped him develop a new approach. As Reich points out: "The actual secrets of the social function of sexual suppression were revealed in the practical experiences afforded me by my sexological work among Viennese adolescents."[29]

Reich worked with student organizations and among the Viennese factory workers. In his lectures, he quickly gave up theoretical presentations on the relationship between Marxism and psychoanalysis or the unconscious, which did not answer his audience's pressing questions. He was also aware of the abstraction and ineffectiveness of Marxist propaganda. The slogans about materialism and revolution did not work. Instead, Reich sought to embrace his audience's cause by taking an interest in them and their daily life. At the end of his lectures, the burning questions flooded in:

> What should one do if one wants to make love and several other people are sleeping in the same room? Why do physicians refuse to help when a woman becomes pregnant and does not want to or cannot have the child? ... [Why is homosexuality punished?] ... My daughter is just seventeen years old and already has a boy friend. Is there anything wrong with that? ... Does the sexual intercourse of an adolescent have any mental consequences?"[30]

Reich tried to respond through the lens of psychoanalysis. His talks focused on topics that concerned his listeners and affected their ordinary lives. He dealt with sexual problems, the education of children, the family: "thousands of people flocked to my meetings to hear what psychoanalysis had to say about social and sexual misery."[31]

The success of Reich's approach—which would continue to grow—was not only due to his charisma, his energy, or his intelligence. There was a sense of distress and expectation among the youth and the workers, and Reich's real strength lay in listening to them. It is likely he owed this particular attitude to the specificity of his practice of analytic therapy. Reich listened and, in contact with these men and women, he learned. He befriended one worker in particular, Zadniker. Zadniker helped him understand that the only questions that mattered were those accessible to everyone. It was also thanks to him that Reich learned about the mental suffering [misère] caused by unemployment. By spending time with the working class, Reich came to challenge the concept of the sublimation of the drives through work: Workers actually suffered in their jobs; in order to bear repetitive factory labor, they were forced to mechanize their behavior. These observations made a large contribution to the development of the concept of "character armor." In fact, to accomplish their task, Reich notes, workers cannot sublimate but must rather "suppress" and "armor" themselves. The material and social conditions of work allow no other destiny for the drive. Reich sums it all up: "Freud's theory of sublimation was correct for research scientists or engineers; it was poorly suited to the average doctor or technician, and altogether unsuitable for work done by the masses."[32]

It was Zadniker, too, who "revealed to [Reich] the deepest secret in the function of marriage and the family: [...] his wife needed him and he needed her as well."[33] Weren't Freud's intuitions—which cast doubt on "civilized sexual morality" and one of its institutions like marriage, asking whether it was worth the "sacrifice it imposed on us"— directly confirmed here by one of those who pays the highest price? Ultimately, Zadniker urged Reich not to take on political responsibilities within the party because it was above all in his medical and educational role that he could act on behalf of the worker's movement, especially for young people and women. Indeed, the masses were all the more prey to poverty and mental illness when they were kept in ignorance. Freud, and Ferenczi after him, had shown that, from the youngest age, people were instilled with a sense of fear and guilt about everything to do with sexuality. Freud even argued that excessive repression generated submissiveness, and promoting abstinence was a clever way of producing "conciliatory and resigned masses." Was it not this excessive repression that Reich found among the young poor people in his care? The work carried out at the six sexual hygiene centers[34]—opened in 1929 after the foundation of the Socialist Society for Sexual Counseling and Sexology to which Reich devoted a great deal of money—largely confirmed these views, and young people and women came in large numbers to seek his advice.

Clinical Experience in the Sexual Hygiene Centers and the Critique of Science

His daily experience in the centers opened his scientist's eyes. He found that, contrary to medical prudery, the "young people" to "protect from sexuality" were in reality adults. They worked hard; they already had sexual partners or asked what they needed to do "to stop being single." Unlike the repressive teacher who hid the truth to consolidate his power, Reich listened to them. He heard that they were looking for love and truth, that they wanted to grow up. With them, Reich notes, the social reality they faced contradicted their legitimate desire in every way. The analyst's work in recognizing this desire made it very easy to overcome the symptoms they suffered from:

> However, a brief explanation of the connections [of the relationship between their nervous disturbances and this wretched manner of "orderly" adolescent sexuality] was all that was necessary to enable the adolescents to grasp the facts immediately [...] It was as if they had been long awaiting the information, as if they had been marching lethargically under a yoke without understanding its meaning. They knew everything about their sexuality; they knew they needed love and stagnated without it. [...] Within a few short months, I learned more about sexology and sociology than I had in ten years of analytic practice.[35]

Reich sought to remove the recurring feelings of guilt regarding their sexuality that he found among them.

When they asked questions about "the danger of sexual intercourse between young people," he burst out laughing and advised them to follow their inclinations. And very often this simple and direct approach helped their neurotic disorders disappear.

Another front in Reich's practice concerned the situation facing women. There again, Freud's comments, which seemed to deal with what he observed on site, were invaluable to him. In fact, he noted that the social situation and poverty affecting women was even worse than with men. Early on, Freud had shown that "excessive repression" and its "burden" "fell" first and foremost, and "without any doubt," on women.[36] As we have seen, he had also shown how repression of the desire for knowledge, particularly for a young girl, created inhibitions in a woman conducive later on to her domination and her preparation for marriage. In 1927, he reiterated his critique. According to him, the physiological arguments put forth to describe women's supposedly constitutional feeble-mindedness compared with men had no basis. "Intellectual atrophy" stemmed from suffering a harsh "early prohibition against turning their thoughts to what would most have interested them—namely, the problems of sexual life."[37] In *Studies in the Psychology of Sex*, Havelock Ellis reported the dramatic cases of young patients who committed suicide when they started menstruating. There had been nothing in their education to instruct them ... or rather everything had certainly been done to convince them of the "dirtiness" of sex in order to get them to submit better to their future husbands. The misunderstanding [méconnaissance] of the drives was part of a repressive educational system against which analysts had long struggled.

For Reich, there was no doubt that the social repression of sexuality was at work and expressed itself in many ways in the patients that came to see him. As an analyst in the sexual hygiene clinics, he could not escape it. Indeed, most of the patients who came to the centers were young girls and pregnant women. And one of the most pervasive forms of misery rampant in Vienna, with which Reich was immediately confronted, was abortion. It took place in appalling sanitary conditions and caused the deaths of thousands of women. Doctors in the Red slums would speak grimly about the "Monday morning hemorrhages," Sunday being the only day workers had off to undergo the procedure. According to Reich's numbers, out of a million abortions performed, 20,000 people died from infection, between 40,000 and 60,000 developed serious health problems, and 8,000 were arrested. It is easy to imagine the traumatic damage of these disastrous procedures. Thus, "from the beginning," Reich advocated for

> the unquestionable right of every woman who was pregnant against her will to have an abortion [...] I sent every woman who had become pregnant unknowingly, or against her will, to doctors who performed the abortion. I knew exactly what I was doing and considered it a matter of course to assume the risk. I always saw before my eyes the well-known hatred of such mothers for their children and did not trouble myself with the concerns of population politicians. I was familiar with

their equivocation and the sociological formulations of their attitudes as well.[38]

As Reich also points out, the doctors who supported such arguments would not have accepted for themselves one hundredth of what they demanded of the population in the name of "morality" and the "birth rate."

This key experience in the clinics would open his eyes and encourage him to question science's ideological role. The severity of the cases he dealt with confirmed his first experiences at the policlinic, but here things were even more critical. What seemed exceptional at the policlinic was revealed to be commonplace in the field of the hygiene centers. According to Reich, none of the women that he and his colleagues treated were in the position to welcome a child. Exhausted, abandoned, suffering from severe neurosis or suicidal depression, most of them "harbored deadly hatred ... against the unborn child."[39] Reich faced extreme situations that challenged his most well-established scientific concepts. He states:

> For two years I was so overwhelmed by the people's sexual misery that the conflict between the scientist and the politician within me grew even more intense. It increased especially when I came into contact, through sex-counseling, with the average Viennese working teen-ager. Although I had become acquainted with pubertal needs much earlier, the cases in the Polyclinic and my private practice seemed pathological exceptions to the rule, in the light of contemporary psychoanalytic thought, this rule being based on the "normally adjusted

> adolescent who has overcome his Oedipus complex and complied with the demands of reality." Almost no one reflected upon the concept of a "normal, healthy adolescent," and even less upon compliance "with the demands of reality." The status quo was simply taken for granted and accepted as unchangeable. It was not questioned, in print or elsewhere.[40]

Confronted with the clinic's daily routine and with social deprivation, Reich understood that the science he had inherited and which had shaped him had to be challenged. Its claims were illegitimate: It advanced its theoretical principles about young people and poor women but knew nothing about the reality it was speaking of. In fact, the clinic had shown Reich that these young adults didn't suffer from "a lack of adaptation to reality" due to an "unconquered Oedipus complex," but that they were simply inhibited from taking the final step towards "a happy love life": "When the forward path toward normal healthy love is blocked, the adolescent reverts to an infantile neurosis which is intensified through increased and simultaneously denied genital desire."[41] Analytic therapy showed the way to resolve the conflict: When the analyst recognized this desire, the inhibition and its symptoms were lifted.

But Reich was not content merely to clarify a decisive technical point in the handling of the transference, he also produced a critique of the ideology surreptitiously at work in science. Knowing the psychological and social realities of disadvantaged populations as well as he did, how could he not question the attitude of the scientists who ignored them and continued to approach their problems in a normative and erroneous way? What could be the value and use of the principle of "necessary adaptation to social reality" the psychiatrist invokes? Why does the theoretician infantilize this youth by "oedipalizing" it, that is, misunderstanding [méconnaissant] its real and objective situation of a socially repressed adult? In the name of the clinic, Reich exposed the hypocrisy of this pseudoscientific attitude; he did so all the more easily as he had himself been prisoner to this attitude for years in his previous practice at the policlinic.

Reich detected this same ideology in his psychoanalytic colleagues: for example, in Theodor Reik and his theory of criminality, taken up by Franz Alexander. The latter had claimed that criminal adults or children became so due to a need for self-punishment. But, Reich asked, how could the children of the Red slums in Vienna, starving and left to fend for themselves, do anything but turn out badly? The issue was as much political as scientific. Ignoring the effects of these patients' miserable social condition on their psychic dynamics led the scientist to reverse the order of causation. If the clinic demonstrated that there was in fact a need for self-punishment, it was only a secondary masochistic formation that had to be explained and not a primitive force that had to be substantiated. Reich points out the fallacy of these concepts: "This saved the trouble of any further questioning. If the analyst failed to cure a patient, it was the death instinct that was responsible. If people committed murder, they did so to get themselves put in jail. Children stole to free themselves from the pressure of a tormenting conscience."[42]

Reich saw Reik's propositions as an exaggerated reworking of the hypothesis of the death instinct proposed by Freud in *Beyond the Pleasure Principle*.[43] The death instinct Reik advanced made it possible to dispense with sociological data about crime, which is presented as the attribute of special personalities that need to be studied—individual morbid anomalies that stand out from the rest of the population by a kind of excess of this instinct. Here the psychoanalyst joins the criminologist in service of the bourgeois order and its police. In his office, well sheltered from reality, he holds forth about the dangerous criminal and the reasons for his confession.[44] By misunderstanding [méconnaissant] the social determinism over the individual, it is only one step before the social deprivation that befalls the subject from the masses is blamed on the subject themselves. Fenichel had already shown how the French analyst René Laforgue's concepts, for example, justified social misery and authoritarianism on the grounds of a supposed sadomasochism in the masses.[45] Along with Fenichel, Reich was one of the first to reveal the distortion of psychoanalysis into psychoanalism in the service of bourgeois ideology.

These crucial theoretical questions must be placed in the European geopolitical context of the end of the 1920s and beginning of the 1930s, during which progressive and revolutionary movements were in retreat while reactionary fascist movements flourished. The scientist's "error" in the order of causation, which naturalized the criminal individual by explaining their acts as a need for self-punishment, or that justified violence against the masses by ascribing a sadomasochistic need to them, didn't go unquestioned: Wasn't this an indirect way of legitimizing the representation of a reactionary social order that was sweeping across Europe by making people think that it is based in nature? In psychoanalism, Thanatos becomes a clever way to eliminate the sexual question and its relation to the overdetermination of social fate but also evacuates the responsibility and involvement of the scientist in relation to these phenomena. At the other end of this position, Reich, like Fenichel, made several trips to revolutionary Russia as part of the fight against fascism and Nazism, in order to find an antidote to its spread among the masses. There he found new inspiration: "Returning from the Soviet Union with encouraging and stimulating impressions, I got down to the task of ascertaining the present-day political meaning of sexual suppression in reactionary society."[46] This research gradually led him to identify a new type of action—feared and hated by the bourgeoisie and its intelligentsia but also misunderstood, even held in contempt, by parties on the left—which would turn out to provide crucial leverage against the rise of fascism and Nazism: the politicization of the sexual question. This direction would also lead him to break with Freud.

The Disagreement with Freud

With the global economic crisis of 1929, the situation in Vienna continued to decline. Johann Schober, then minister of foreign affairs, chancellor, and head of the Austrian police, was well known for his violence.[47] The social democrats in the coalition he led went from compromise to compromise. They passed emergency laws that destroyed the republic's achievements. For their part, the communists denounced these abuses and advocated civil war. But they were a minority and no longer able to rally the masses. The rise of fascism in Austria seemed inevitable.

Facing the climate of fear and distrust setting in, Reich continued his analytic reflection. He sought to unravel the fear he witnessed spreading among the masses in his daily practice. He observed that while the social democratic party still enjoyed approval, it was precisely for emotional reasons: It felt like a home for the homeless. In his view, this was why the slogan "communists want to sow division and discord" worked. The communist organizations' blindness was catastrophic. The party leaders had a purely political and ideological vision of class consciousness, even though their abstract understanding of social processes was continually belied by facts. The masses were tempted by fascism; while the supposedly inevitable realization of proletarian revolution slipped away, the communist leaders continued to explain the advance of fascism as a result of the masses being lied to. But, Reich asked, how could the attraction to fascism or Nazism be based on "lies" alone?

Yet, Reich's critique of the Communist Party and its strategy did not prevent him from organizing within the party. He participated in demonstrations, distributed newspapers, and supported comrades under attack. In September 1929, he traveled one last time to revolutionary Russia, where he tried to convince the Communist Academy officials of psychoanalysis's value for Marxism.[48]

But psychoanalysis had already long been discredited. A veritable Thermidor had buried the Russian sexual revolution. Stalin's promotion of a return to the family and patriarchal order was well underway. Even though Reich showed his doubts at the time, he could not assess the gravity of the situation. Nothing essential seemed to distinguish Stalin's reaction from the fascist or Nazi reaction, nor from their propaganda exalting the family and fatherland.

On December 12, 1929, Reich gave a presentation of his ideas to Freud's inner circle, where he showed the link between prevention of neurosis and the political critique of the family. He scandalized the gathering around Freud with his questions:

> Is it normal that 60 to 80% of young people suffer from neurotic disorders? Is it normal that out of 70% of patients, only a mere 30% can have recourse to psychoanalysis? What roles do education, morality, and the capitalist system play in the genesis of this psychic misery? Finally, is it surprising that 80% of Viennese workers, who live with their families in a single room, suffer from sexual conflicts and inhibitions?

These questions were received as provocations. Freud responded harshly to Reich that it was not psychoanalysis's job to "save the world." He recognized Reich's clinical talent but rejected the practical consequences of his critique of the family. From notes by Sterba, who was present that day, Freud disapproved of Reich's "therapeutic ambition": "the scientific investigator … should not take therapy into consideration." He also expressed his disillusionment with Reich's social ambitions, and for his part seemed to have given up any hope for radical reforms: "I said everything about it once in an earlier essay. [Freud was referring to his paper, "'Civilized' Sexual Morality and Modern Nervous Illness," published in 1908.] There I expressed the sharpest criticism of our sexual morality. But all suggestions of reforming the situation fail."[49] At that time, a decisive argument for the history of psychoanalysis was growing in importance: that it was not a worldview, a *Weltanschauung*. The aim was to protect it from any ideological recuperation—which in no way prevented the analyst's political commitment.[50] This argument, which Reich embraced at the time, turned against him. We'll come back to this.

According to Reich, *Civilization and Its Discontents*, which would soon be published, in 1930, contained whole sections of Freud's objections to him from that day. The book is without question a radically pessimist turning point in Freud's views on culture and humanity. For his part, Reich published his ideas at the same time in *Sexual Maturity, Abstinence, Marital Morals*.

Again these two books and the opposing positions they express—pessimistic withdrawal versus radical commitment—are to be seen in relation to the threatening sociopolitical context in which their authors lived. Their near contemporary releases reflect a crisis in psychoanalysis itself, which sought, by opposing paths, to extend a fate in the process of darkening and closing. If a certain historiography of psychoanalysis likes to show that Reich's path of "political commitment" is an institutional dead end (a few years later Reich was expelled from the IPA), and says nothing about his relative future success as a militant analyst in the worker's movement, it puts much less emphasis on the disastrous practical perspective that Freud's position authorizes: In his new view of culture, the impact of political violence against the masses is largely downplayed. The weight of violence is now carried above all by humanity's irredeemably aggressive nature. From then on, the analyst no longer had to take a position.

Sexual Repression and the Critique of the Communist Party

Reich decided to leave Vienna for Berlin, where a more progressive political climate still existed. Fromm, Bernfeld, and Fenichel—like most of the analysts who participated in the "Children's Seminar" (which gathered the third generation of Berlin analysts)—were supportive of his work. At this time, Reich had not yet officially broken with Freud, who assured him in a letter that he would keep his position in Vienna.[51]

In Berlin, Reich also joined the Communist Party. But there, too, he experienced the same difficulties and the same impasses [apories] as in Vienna. Moreover, the political situation was rapidly worsening. The Nazi Party's success was staggering: Its votes went from 800,000 in 1926, to 6,500,000 in 1930. Meanwhile, the communists were in trouble, their propaganda was abstract and disembodied. Above all, they tried to gain a foothold on their opponents' terrain, which doomed them to failure. For example, the Communist Party organized military processions in the countryside, but the Nazis were much better at this, and their processions were a great success. It was "so conspicuous," Reich said, "that I was amazed at how little attention our people paid it."[52] The troops making up the Nazi processions were recruited from local reactionary groups. How, then, could the peasants view parades under the banner of a far too distant international? The sexual and emotional component of political movements and its intertwining with the daily life of the masses completely escaped the Communist Party cadres. To regain control, the Marxists would have had to conduct their own self-critique and analyze the opposing propaganda. They would have then understood how and why the Nazi Party found a favorable response from the masses where theirs had failed, and on what suitable terrain to focus their efforts.

This is what Reich set out to do early on. In his 1933 book *Mass Psychology of Fascism*, he showed that the success of Nazi propaganda was explained by its understanding and manipulation—even unconsciously—of the mass's psychic reactions.[53] Nazi propaganda took up old themes present in bourgeois culture, like racial and national purity, the denunciation of the enemy as Jew or Bolshevik, the promotion of the German family, and a return to military order. These themes, embedded in the culture and each individual, were powerful emotional motifs that the Nazis used to capture the masses, playing on the sexual anxiety they were burdened with. From this point of view, the Marxist argument of "class interest" sounded quite disembodied and out of place. How could they reach individuals, how could they convince them to move towards a hypothetical revolution that was such a distant prospect, so uncertain and so risky in terms of their present life? Contrary to the claims of the doctrine, the workers were not revolutionary in themselves, and it was not enough to explain the theory of history in pamphlets to make them become so.

Reich observed that a rigid formalism prevailed in everyday communist practice, perceptible in the climate of militant meetings. During a meeting in Berlin where more than 20,000 workers gathered in a feverish atmosphere after a demonstration involving several deaths, a party cadre managed to freeze the mood by giving a presentation on the German bourgeoisie's budget. At the communist youth meetings Reich attended, the party cadres quibbled over how to approach the youth, but the pamphlets they produced were abstract and of interest to no one. The correctness and rationality of their arguments were not enough to set the masses in motion *libidinally*, Reich noted. His psychoanalytic experience was decisive here. He told the story of a worker who had been a very active militant in the Communist Party, who then went over to the Nazi Party. A mechanic well known by his comrades, he was part of the same brigade as Reich, but during the 1932 elections, he went to the other side. His old comrades spat in his face and called him a traitor. But Reich says, "He was not especially different from the others."[54] Libidinal interest did not necessarily intersect with class interest; Lenin himself understood this, Reich points out, when, in defiance of theory and to win the revolution, he promised land to the peasants—even if it was a "petty bourgeois" promise that the theory disavowed since it went against collectivization and, moreover, since the peasant class was not expected to carry out the revolution. Reich's views on the contradiction that could exist within the masses, or on the force of desire that pushed them towards Nazism rather than communism, were completely incomprehensible to the party cadres. When Reich pointed out that the SA (*Sturmabteilung*; the Nazi Party storm troopers spreading terror) was made up of workers and employees, they retorted that this was a reactionary idea. For the communists, the objective progress of the historical process and economic development guaranteed that the masses would become revolutionary and fight Hitler, the representative of Capital. But the opposite was happening: These so-called experts in the meaning of history were disproven on their own turf – the masses they defended were going to vote overwhelmingly for Hitler. There were even going to *desire* the Führer.

Reich had reached a decisive theoretical stage in his psychoanalytic understanding of the masses and the grip that reactionary political forces exerted on them. As in a bourgeois regime, but to a much greater degree in the Nazi and Stalin dictatorships, sexual repression was at the very source of reactionary power:

> Political reaction, with fascism and the church at its head, demands that the masses should renounce happiness here on earth; it demands chastity, obedience, self-denial, sacrifice for the nation, the people, the fatherland. The problem is not that the reactionaries demand this, but that the masses, by complying with these demands, are supporting the reactionaries and allowing them to enrich themselves and extend their power. The reac-

tionaries take advantage of the guilt feelings of mass individuals, of their ingrained modesty, their tendency to suffer privation silently and willingly, sometimes even happily, and they take advantage of their identification with the glorious Führer, whose "love of the people" is for them a substitute for any real satisfaction of their needs.[55]

From then on, for Reich, the sexual repression exerted on everyday life by reactionary forces became the object of true struggle. Once liberated, sexual energy would allow for the realization of the power necessary for true revolution. The bourgeois science of the individual was thus definitively overturned: The problem was not knowing why among the repressed mass some rare, isolated individuals rebelled, were antisocial, or stole but rather why the majority consented, approved, and even desired this repression they were subjected to. Or as Reich wrote, "We persist in believing that the fundamental problem of a correct psychological doctrine is not why a hungry man steals but the exact opposite: Why doesn't he steal?"[56] Science no longer served social reaction but political revolution. By lifting the inhibition that struck the masses and restoring the sexual function that had been denied to them, the prevention of current neuroses was going to allow the subject to regain its freedom and power to act.

This is the measure of the theoretical path travelled by Reich, and its practical consequences. It is also clear why it was not followed by Freud, who probably considered the situation to be unfavorable, as we will see in the next chapter.

The Politicization of Sexual Life and the Success of Sexpol

In a 1930 paper addressed to the World League for Sexual Reform, Reich summarized the results of his work in the Viennese clinics. The league brought together all the organizations and figures who sought to promote progress in sexual matters (decriminalization of homosexuality, right to abortion, women's rights, etc.), but in an apolitical manner. The league had invited Freud and he declined the offer. Its members, who were generally involved in politics, or even in political parties, wanted the associations they were active in to remain independent. In Germany, the league had more than 350,000 members—that is, more than any political party—and a significant portion of its members supported the revolutionary perspective. In his paper, Reich proposed a platform for the league; based on his experience in the clinics, he sought to politicize the sexual problem on a large scale. His aim was to unite all of these associations in order to reach the masses and effectively combat the rise of Nazism. The league rejected Reich's proposals but, against all expectations, the German Communist Party accepted his project and put him in charge of a new, unified structure. Eight associations of the league immediately answered the call.[57] Thus was born the German Association for Proletarian Sexual Politics, known as Sexpol, which held its first congress in Düsseldorf in 1931.

In a few months, Sexpol went from 20,000 members to more than 40,000. Reich organized conferences and meetings, applying his method: Far from the catechisms of communist propaganda, and steeped in his experience in Vienna, he knew that the starting point had to be people's real-life situations, that is, the repression they endure. In reality, the average worker "is neither a clear-cut revolutionary nor a clear-cut conservative, but stands divided" due to the social situation: "his psychic structure derives on the one hand from the social situation (which prepares the ground for revolutionary attitudes) and on the other hand from the entire atmosphere of authoritarian society—the two being at odds with one another."[58] It is therefore ineffective to emphasize class consciousness and demand that the masses join the communists in the name of the historical rationality of the revolutionary movement. This means completely ignoring the real lives of the masses. Yet it is precisely the concrete, everyday life of the workers (work, food, housing, raising a family, going out, etc.), made up of constraints of all kinds, that explains their class consciousness as "partially undeveloped and partially interfused with contrary reactionary structural elements."[59] Life, with its countless facets and necessities, obviously has a greater impact than any political propaganda.

In a 1934 pamphlet, *What Is Class Consciousness?*, Reich reverses the perspective and advocates that the "enlightened party cadre" listen to the "average person":

This essay should be read as an appeal by average, nonpolitical men to the future leaders of the revolution—an appeal for a better understanding, with a little less insistence on a grasp of the "historical process"; for a more adequate articulation of their real problems and desires;

for a less theoretical grasp of the "subjective factor" in history; and for a better practical understanding of what this factor represents in the life of the masses.[60]

With their strictly rationalist perspective, the Party cadres and its "vanguard" were blind to the real psychic and material processes that mobilized the masses and could lead them to an effective political changeover. For Reich, the vanguard had to come down from its pedestal, to become more humble, and to listen to the masses they needed to learn from. It was necessary to return to the question of their everyday concerns in order to tie "high politics" to "small personal life." Reich had learned this from his experience with the poor of Vienna. He knew that the alienation Marx described was not something abstract: It was lodged in the thousand-and-one details of life itself. So it was necessary to intervene on this level, not from "on high," the antithesis of the classic way promoted by the party.

Reich gave an overview of his ideas when he spoke at the Berlin Marxist Worker's School in 1931:

> In practical work among the uneducated, and usually politically disinterested, members of these organizations, only one type of approach could possibly lead to success, namely, gaining human confidence through personal warmth, avoiding all theorizing, and awakening an awareness of personal needs, whether large or small. Once this was accomplished, socialistic objectives became a foregone conclusion. From the very beginning I recognized the uselessness of the political brochures of party organizations.[61]

Analyzing alienation with those who were the most exposed to it developed a class consciousness far more consistent, far more libidinally inscribed in the subject than that promoted by a slogan. Analyzing and recognizing alongside the workers "the progressive desires, ideas and thought" but also "the desires, fears, thoughts and ideas"[62] that prevent them from expressing themselves: Only then would the libidinal power of Nazism and its demonstrations be deflated and the true revolution would find the power of its realization. This was the politicization of the sexual question.

In Berlin, Dresden, Stettin, and Leipzig, the workers came to see Reich. His pamphlets and those of his friends met with a resounding response. Reich published *The Sexual Struggle of Youth*, then *The Invasion of Compulsory Sexual Morality*; Annie Reich, his wife, produced pamphlets for parents (*When Your Child Asks Questions*) and also for children, such as *Adults' Secrets Revealed to Children*. Soon, Sexpol's ideas won over the factories in the Ruhr, a region then dominated by the nationalists. The success was such that members of the Hitler Youth and Catholic Youth quit their organizations to join those of the Communist Party.

This victory, which confirmed Reich's views and method, paradoxically marks the beginning of his troubles with the Communist Party. The party cadres were worried. Disconnected from the youth, how could they accommodate these National Socialist women who joined Sexpol organizations en masse and asked questions about sexuality? The leadership of the Communist Party in Berlin accused Reich of wanting to replace economic politics with sexual politics. The sexual struggle, according to them, was completely secondary to the class struggle: Wasn't it, moreover, a petty-bourgeois struggle? The Communist Party sought to regain control and called for meetings to bring the Sexpol organizations into compliance with its vision. From then on, the party was in direct political and organizational conflict with the noncommunist members of the sexual reform associations. Reich's books and pamphlets were banned in the communist youth movements—a ban that was obviously not respected. Later, the party got stirred up: The Dresden communist youth organizations asked for housing for each adolescent. Reich had to appear before a party commission, but he slipped away after placing his best disciples in key positions in the organization.

The burning of the Reichstag interrupted the matter. The Nazis were responsible, but they accused the communists. Thus, with Hindenburg's indirect complicity, 1,500 communist intellectuals and officials were arrested by the SA. Many of Reich's friends were executed, and he himself owed his salvation only to the fact that he was never an official member of the German Communist Party and he did not appear on the SA's lists.

So began his exile. In the spring of 1933, he traveled to Copenhagen, where he received the support of Leunbach, one of the founders of the league who shared his ideas. But he was not well regarded by the authorities, who did not renew his residence permit. In the autumn of 1933, he reached Malmö in Sweden, where he was regularly joined by his friends and students from Copenhagen. Intrigued by these movements, the police surveilled him and searched his house without a warrant. In Sweden too, his papers were not renewed. Reich returned to Denmark illegally in June 1934, before finally settling in Oslo, Norway, at the end of October 1934. He stayed there until 1939. While in Oslo, he founded *The Political Psychology and Sex Economy Review*, which had correspondents around the world. Reich presented his theses in this journal and reflected on the organization of the working world. He began his critique of bureaucracy, drawing from his own experience of the Communist Party and the IPA. In a 1937 reprint of *The Sexual Struggle of Youth*, he even came to repudiate the terms "communism" and "communist," which, "following the catastrophic attitude of the Comintern," had lost their meaning. He proposed replacing them with the word "revolutionary." According to him, his book sticks to "the first communist league founded by Marx." He reproached himself for not being able to conceive earlier on the organization of another movement based on self-management: "The term 'Sexpol' had been introduced long before and signified the 'organization of sex-politics,' although it had no presidents and secretaries [...] It would not have been consistent with the issues [...] However, applying the concept of self-government in forming an organization was rewarding." Wasn't this a libertarian third way that could bring about the revolution better than the Soviet and psychoanalytic bureaucracies? Reich no longer looked to the East. He committed himself to a critique of the Soviet model in order to elucidate the reasons for its collapse and reversal. He now turned his attention to the Spanish revolution, which offered "a good lesson to the revolutionary movement and bourgeois democracy."[63]

3
The Future of Freudian Pessimism

As we have seen, from 1918 to 1927, Freud promoted an optimistic political vision, in favor of progressive reforms.[1] Psychoanalysis and its new institutions, like the policlinics whose movement he initiated, contributed to these reforms. In *The Future of an Illusion* (1927), Freud still defended a vision of education where social constraint must be desacralized and replaced by an approach based on facts and rationality, which should lead to "love of man" and "decrease of suffering."[2] In this book, he also justifies the mass revolt against oppression by a minority and denounces the fate of women.

But during the summer of 1929, while writing *Civilization and Its Discontents* (which would be published in 1930), Freud changed course. His critique of illusion was no longer limited to religion but extended to communism. In contrast to his previously open position, his verdict was now final. Furthermore, Freud insisted more and more on the idea of psychoanalysis's "neutrality." This idea, already clearly present in Freud's conception before 1929, can be summarized this way: As a science, psychoanalysis does not have to take political sides. It is not a *Weltanschauung*, a worldview. However, its discoveries do indeed have effects on the world and on politics. There is thus a whole field of psychoanalytic social applications—what is classically called applied psychoanalysis—but this field is articulated on the basis of needs brought to light by psychoanalytic science. Psychoanalysis could be extended (removed from the context of the couch and the cure), but only following its own logic and not partisan considerations. Although he was committed to the left (for example, when he supported Victor Adler), Freud was always determined to preserve the field of psychoanalysis from ideological recuperations.

The Context of Freud's Reversal: The End of the Hope in Russia and the Rise of Nazism

Due to the political context, Freud's idea of psychoanalysis as an independent and neutral science would actually experience an unprecedented dominance in the analytic field after the publication of *Civilization and Its Discontents*—witness the flourishing of texts by psychoanalysts on this theme—but it would also undergo a very clear shift.[3] With the collapse of the revolutionary ideal and the rise of Stalinism and fascism, this debate which had up to then been secondary, now became decisive. The result would be a new orientation towards a simply *apolitical* conception of psychoanalysis.

So what happened that could explain such a radical shift in the link between psychoanalysis and politics in Freud's work?[4] To understand this, we must return to the geopolitical context of that moment. Using only theoretical positions to interpret these texts ignores the historical and material conditions in which they were written. Beyond individual positions, we see a real crisis for psychoanalysis,

Figure 3 From left to right, in the first row: Sigmund Freud, G. Stanley Hall, Carl Gustav Jung; in the second row: Abraham A. Brill, Ernest Jones, Sándor Ferenczi. Photograph taken in September 1909, during a series of lectures at Clark University (Massachusetts)

which required a rethinking of the link between psychoanalysis and politics, and created a split in the discipline.

While, as late as 1927, Freud still joined Reich in defending the experiment of the Russian Revolution in *The Future of an Illusion*, this was no longer the case in 1929. They both had in common a certain misunderstanding of the real situation in the USSR: If they failed to perceive the authoritarian takeover that had long since crushed Lenin's left and the first progressive reformers,[5] we have to admit that Freud opened his eyes before Reich did. As opposed to Reich, Freud did not need to travel to

Russia to see the failure of the revolutionary experiment. He knew the psychoanalysts of the Moscow Institute personally—Sabina Spielrein, J. D. Ermakoff, and Mosche Wulff, who certainly made him aware of the deteriorating situation in their country. At the beginning of the 1930s, Reich critiqued the Russian experiment in turn. In fact, Stalin's bureaucratic stranglehold began its work as soon as Lenin's decline in 1923, culminating in a veritable "sexual thermidor."[6] Vera Schmidt's psychoanalytic children's home was closed at the beginning of this period (1924). The hunt for "Trotskyist contraband"—presented as the last official support of psychoanalysis—and Stalin's promotion of a return to the family and patriarchal authority as the nation's foundation would ring the final death knell for the already residual emancipatory movements and for Russian psychoanalysis alike. This context allows Freud's political turning point to make sense. And here, too, light can be shed on the sharp shift expressed in *Civilization and Its Discontents*, where he links social violence *primarily* to the necessary deprivations imposed by the process of culture, and where he condemns communism. But does this discernment regarding the disaster of the Russian experiment, as well as the decline of progressive movements in the face of the rise of fascism, mean throwing out the baby with the bathwater, as Freud seems to be doing? Reich will not take the same position; this difference is a decisive factor in the link between psychoanalysis and politics, and the discipline's immediate future.

It is in this concrete historical context that we must understand what is called "Freud's pessimism," often associated with his "realism," and promoted by contemporary psychoanalysis. In the principle of a death instinct embodied [hypostasié] by the whole of culture, as present in *Civilization*, contemporary psychoanalysis sees a posteriori the expression of Freud's theoretical genius and his political "lucidity" with regard to the coming destructive war. But once again, causality is reversed.[7] The fact that the principle reaches its theoretical peak when the tide is turning towards social barbarism should, however, raise questions. The Western European progressive movements were no longer rallying people, antisemitism was gaining ground everywhere. Freud "no longer nurtures a great hope for the future." The attempt of revolutionary Russia he had believed in, one of whose objectives was to achieve the nonreligious education he wished for, was closed up in violent authoritarianism. Freud then seems to apply literally what he had already declared in *The Future of an Illusion*: "Should the experiment prove unsatisfactory I am ready to give up the reform and to return to my earlier, purely descriptive judgement that man is a creature of weak intelligence who is ruled by his instinctual wishes."[8] It is in this context that we must understand Freud's reference to Hobbes's maxim (*Homo homini lupus*), and the fact that he supports the thesis that social problems and their attendant violence are *first and foremost* a structural fact of the human psyche, characterized by an "aggressive tendency." Sick[9] and jaded, Freud gave in to the geopolitical situation of the moment: "The time comes when each one of us has to give up as illusions the expectations which, in his youth, he pinned upon his fellow men, and when he may learn how much difficulty and pain has been added to his life by their ill-will."[10] Freud's avowed pessimism is tinged with nostalgia and disillusionment. The peak it reaches must therefore be all the more circumscribed by this period.[11] Failure to recognize this fact leads to a misinterpretation of *Civilization and Its Discontents* and its place within Freud's oeuvre[12] but also in the history of the discipline: For this turning point symbolically marks not only a before and after in Freud's theory but also in psychoanalytic practice. Indeed, had it been elaborated in the 1920s, this theoretical pessimism could never have given rise to anything of the breadth and fruitfulness shown by psychoanalysis at the time. The moment that Freud announces this pessimism in 1930 also marks the beginning of the slow decline of the psychoanalytic movement, to which, in a way, it made a major contribution. It is not just a moment of disillusionment—all the greater given the high level of hope and energy invested—it also opens another phase for psychoanalysis, which will gradually lead to disaster. The new perspective on politics—called "realist," but in reality totally cynical—must be seen in relation to the practices orchestrated by Ernest Jones in order to "rescue" the discipline, an endeavor that Freud would soon support.

Ernest Jones, The "Savior" of Psychoanalysis

A Welsh psychiatrist and psychoanalyst, Ernest Jones was the representative of English-speaking psychoanalysis within the IPA. In 1911, he founded the American Psychoanalytic Association, and in 1919, the British Psychoanalysis Society. He is also known for *The Life and Work of Freud*,[13] his biography of Freud (really a hagiography that is still a reference in many psychoanalytic circles), in which he presents his version of the psychoanalytic movement's history.

Under the pretext of the collapse of the revolutionary movement on the old continent, Jones, who was not very favorable to leftist Freudians, intended to revisit the link between psychoanalysis and politics and redirect it towards a more "reasonable" perspective, towards liberalism or bourgeois parliamentarism as practiced in English-speaking countries. At the moment when the situation of continental psychoanalysis was poised to become catastrophic with the rise of fascism—in the same countries where shortly before it had experienced remarkable growth—a new strategy took shape: to shift its center of gravity to the English-speaking axis, and make it more discreet, particularly in Germany and Austria, in order to "protect" it. Against most of his disciples' wishes, Freud came to support the idea that "psychoanalysis's existence as an organization must continue under the same conditions under the Third Reich."[14] Jones became the instigator of this "rescue" policy.

This new direction led to a number of consequences. In the first place, it would be necessary to "remove" the analysts who were too vocal on the left. This was precisely the case with Reich who, at the beginning of the 1930s, had acquired great notoriety through his work with the masses and his publications. In the eyes of the German and Austrian public, he seemed to be the voice of a young up-and-coming psychoanalysis. He was well known enough to be a target for the Nazis, whom he criticized openly. Therefore, Reich now posed a threat for the discipline and its survival. But contrary to Jones's version, of history, his was not an isolated case, as most analysts at the time were clearly on the left. Reich's secret expulsion from the IPA in the summer of 1933 rang the official death knell for the political commitment of all analysts but also heralded the coming racialization of the Berlin Institute: Soon, all the Jews would in turn be expelled. Of course, they were rather, as Jones puts it, "invited to leave." The great voices of 1920s psychoanalysis (mostly Jewish and left-wing) would end up going into exile: Eitingon, Fenichel, Simmel, and many others.

This twofold movement of expulsion took place under cover of the same argument, that of psychoanalysis as "apolitical." As president of the association during this period, Jones made it the constitutive and immutable rule of the psychoanalytic discipline. As mentioned, this topic was having unprecedented success. Between 1929 and 1933, no less than five texts were devoted to it, including Freud's 1933 text, "The Question of a *Weltanshcauung*."[15] Under the guise of a scholarly discussion, this text actually involves major political stakes that affect the fate of psychoanalysis as a practice. At a time when Nazism was in full swing, Freud reaffirms in this text the idea of a neutral psychoanalysis.

What Nazism Did to Psychoanalysis: Eitingon's Departure

One month after Hitler seized power, Max Eitingon, the director of the Berlin Psychoanalytic Institute, got worried. Eitingon was the founder and main financial backer of the institute, with which he (rightly) identified; in 1930 Ernest Jones considered him "the heart of the entire international psychoanalytic movement." But, as he was both Polish and Jewish, he did not have German citizenship. Above all, he disagreed with the new political direction taken by psychoanalysis. For him, any idea of adapting psychoanalysis or the institute to Nazism was inane. And in the calamitous political circumstances of the time, no one could purport to replace him as the head of the institute without betraying its spirit. He asserted with determination: He would only leave if compelled by force. Besides, they had not yet received any official state directives on the subject, and should there be any, Eitingon simply planned to close the institute. He considered himself the last bastion against the barbarism that could take psychoanalysis over. His position could not be clearer: There could be no connection and no compromise with the Nazi enemy, and it would be unworthy and dishonorable to anticipate such a move. He wrote to Freud along these lines on March 19, 1933, to explain his point of view and to ask him, in return, to take a stand:

> I would indeed love to wait and see how things evolve, to wait quietly to see what might happen to the Psychoanalytic Institute. To be there to the last moment, eventually to close it myself if it was necessary to close it, or at least be there if it were closed. As I can't think of anyone who would be able to continue it in the same spirit, in such different circumstances, I would like to leave it to no one; if this absurd situation were to arise, to see to it that the Institutes survives, while I, a foreigner and doctor, am no longer be able to work. Would

I be doing an injustice to my local colleagues if, in such a transformed situation, I no longer believed in any continuity, however approximate, in the survival of the Institute, if I were forced one day to leave my workplace and the country where I have lived for forty years? I use this word literally: forced, because I wouldn't dream of leaving a second earlier or under less pressure than that. So many of my colleagues have already been dismissed in recent years, how many others would stop, or would still be forced to stop, and then again, I probably have the right to identify myself with the Institute, or conversely, to identify the Institute with myself. A few colleagues here have responded with incomprehension or rejection when I've alluded to these ideas, all of which doesn't dissuade me from sticking my point of view. I would love to know your opinion, Herr Doktor.[16]

Despite the censorship imposed on his correspondence with Freud after 1933 and the need for the two letter writers to nuance their words, Eitingon's letter is explicit and radical. Although he does not name them, the colleagues who rejected his ideas were well known to Freud: Ernest Jones, Felix Boehm, and Carl Müller-Braunchsweig, psychoanalyst members of the association who sought to oust him. According to the new "rescue" policy, the leaders of psychoanalysis must necessarily be Aryan in order to comply with the requirements of the new power. And this was precisely the case for Boehm and Müller-Braunschweig, which is the reason why Jones sought to promote them—something Eitingon would not accept.

Freud quickly responded on March 21, 1933, presenting him with three possibilities that revealed his own inclination towards the solution rejected by his disciple. Of course, Freud considered the administrative closure of the institute: "First, psychoanalysis is banned and the Institute is subjected to administrative closure." But, unlike Eitingon, Freud also saw two other possibilities for continuation. He did not heed Eitingon's warning that insisted it would be impossible to continue the institute's activities without seriously corrupting its spirit. On the contrary, he envisioned the institute's survival under Eitingon's unofficial leadership:

> Second, nothing happens to the Institute, but as a foreigner, etc. you are removed from its leadership. You remain in Berlin, however, and can continue to exert an unofficial influence. In this case, I think you could keep the Institute open ... It is also in the general interest that it be preserved to survive adverse times.

In this respect, Freud was completely blind. He continues: "In the meantime, an indifferent person like Boehm could continue to lead it."[17] But Boehm was anything but "indifferent"; he was an "Aryan," recognized by the new German state as "racially pure." Eitingon was not fooled by this proposal and responded to Freud three days later: "The possibility I feared was precisely that we might be forced to submit the Institute to an 'indifferent' person, and that this 'indifferent' person might be just such a person as you named."[18] History would prove him right: A few years later, Boehm would prove to be a very zealous "psychoanalyst," actively collaborating in the surveillance of homosexuals and their deportation.[19]

Freud did consider a third possibility: The institute survived, but Eitingon left, voluntarily or forced, and "lost all influence." For Freud, a "peril was growing within the Institute," and it could be co-opted by internal enemies for their "own purposes." He mentions by name Harald Shultz-Hencke, a non-Jewish dissident psychoanalyst who could appear credible in the Nazi's eyes. Reading this third option, we understand that for Freud, unlike Eitingon, the greatest peril for psychoanalysis and the institute was not Nazism, which both must be able to adapt to, but their co-optation by dissidents who would distort its spirit! In his letter to Eitingon on April 17, 1933, in which he recounts his meeting with Boehm, Freud points out that just like Müller-Braunschweig, Boehm "[refused] any essential concession in the functioning of analysis."[20] According to him, "the essence of analysis" (which should be defined) could survive under the conditions of Nazism; the main threat would primarily come from seditious individuals within the field. In these dark hours, Freud seemed more concerned with preserving the temple of psychoanalysis than considering the general political situation. The third possibility was thus clearly a "deterrent." In fact, Freud indirectly invited Eitingon to choose the second option: Keep the Berlin Psychoanalytic Institute open and "withdraw" from its presidency in favor of Boehm, supposedly to preserve its "essence." When they met, Boehm assured Freud that "Schultz Hencke will never be part of the office," but also—at Freud's request—that he would work to have Reich expelled.[21] Although Freud had never held Boehm in high esteem, these few guarantees seemed enough to earn him his trust.

Despite the threat of Nazism, Reich continued to openly express his opinions, which the new approach found unacceptable. In the early 1930s, in addition to his work at Sexpol, he had the "cheek" (Anna Freud's word)[22] to return to Vienna to give a lecture at the Psychoanalytic Society, where he publicly presented his political commitment against the Nazis. In *Mass Psychology of Fascism*, published in 1933, he openly critiqued National Socialism. In that same year, as we have seen, Freud published his article "The Question of a *Weltanschauung*," which asks whether psychoanalysis is a worldview and, of course, responds in the negative.[23] This text is not insignificant. As opposed to today's mainstream analytic reading, it is not just a question of epistemology. In the midst of the rise of Nazism, Freud defends the idea of the neutrality of psychoanalytic science. Under the guise of a scientific discussion, Freud designates as adversaries, after religion, political anarchism (the "counterpart" of relativism in science) and Marxism. As for the latter, his judgement is final:

> The other opposition has to be taken far more seriously, and in this instance I feel the liveliest regret at the inadequacy of my information. I suspect that you know more about this business than I do and that you took up your position long ago in favour of Marxism or against it ... Theoretical Marxism, as realized in Russian Bolshevism, has acquired the energy and the self-contained and exclusive character of a Weltanschauung, but at the same time an uncanny likeness to what it is fighting against.[24]

Freud dismisses Marxism as a dangerous *Weltanschauung*, far removed from psychoanalytic science and unrelated to it. Just after the overwhelming success of the Nazis, he made no public critique of them, and instead explicitly targeted communism. The political subtext was clear: The aim was to counter the idea of a politically committed psychoanalysis. For the new line of "rescuing psychoanalysis," Reich's position was unacceptable and threatened the "survival" of analytic institutions.[25] His secret expulsion[26] from the German Psychoanalytic Society took place during the summer of 1933. And it was also in name of this neutrality that the Aryanization of the institute was cemented.

"Neutrality" in Psychoanalysis and Aryanization of the German Psychoanalytic Society

In 1933, Max Eitingon opposed the appointment of Boehm as president of the German Psychoanalytic Institute, just as he disapproved of Reich's expulsion.[27] This resolute socialist left Germany for Israel [Palestine], where he opened a policlinic based on the Berlin model. In Berlin, Boehm and Müller-Braunschweig were finally elected to the management of the institute on November 18, 1933. Werner Kemper, another "Aryan" analyst, was elected as the auditor. Soon, this triumvirate reigned supreme, and meanwhile the Jews and the Reds were driven out at a session chaired by Jones himself.

As Boehm noted in a report to Jones, he went with Müller-Braunschweig to the National Socialist minister of culture to demonstrate that psychoanalysis was not "Jewish-Marxist filth." Prompted by a civil servant to draw a distinction between true psychoanalysis and its leftist deviations, Müller-Braunschweig wrote a memorandum that was read to Jones. An abridged version of it was published in a Nazi propaganda newspaper, the *Reichswart*, in October 1933. In it, Müller-Braunschweig defended the argument that psychoanalysis was not a *Weltanschauung*, thus rejecting the idea that it was "disintegrating the German soul." If it were to prove to be "dangerous" in the hands of a "destructive mind, it still has a role to play in helping build the Nazi regime." As the historian Geoffrey Cocks notes, this essay "indirectly but clearly"[28] condemns his Jewish colleagues—and we might add, just as clearly, the analysts on the left, with Reich at the forefront. In an official letter, Reich denounced Müller-Braunschweig's message, just as he courageously denounced the German Psychoanalytic Society's collusion with Hitler's regime:

> As a member of the DPG [German Psychoanalytic Society] forced to emigrate, I hereby declare that Müller-Braunschweig's article in question is a disgrace to all of psychoanalytic science and the movement. Under the leadership of his board of directors, the DPG attempts to integrate psychotherapy into the German Society for General Medicine, although the *Reichsführer* declares in a foreword to the December 1933 *Zentralblatt für Psychotherapie*: "the Society expects all of its members who write to have studied Adolf Hitler's fundamental book *Mein Kampf* and to consider it to be a primary work."[29]

Over and above Müller-Braunschweig's ideological position, and in keeping with the new "rescue" direction, the German Psychoanalytic Society's aim was to integrate psychotherapy into the German Society of General Medicine, which required its members to pledge allegiance to the Führer. Encouraged by Jones, Boehm actively pursued this institutional merger.

In 1934, during the 23rd International Congress of Psychoanalysis in Lucerne, protest was rumbling among analysts against the recent direction taken by the German Psychoanalytic Society. Aware of this state of mind, Jones, in his capacity as president of the IPA, publicly defended Boehm:

> I heard some very harsh opinions expressed in ignorance of these facts, which is enough to prove that irrational factors are at work. I would simply add that Dr. Boehm first visited Professor Freud personally in April '33, in order to prevent the clashes and criticism that were bound to follow; from the outset, he gave me, in my capacity as president, a faithful account of all of events in the personal talks.

And to conclude: "I have reason to hope that Dr. Boehm's services to psychoanalysis will survive any criticism to which he might temporarily be exposed."[30] Psychoanalysts who had long been involved in political struggles were stunned by the new official leadership. At the congress, Reich's book *Mass Psychology of Fascism* was banned from display.[31] Reich, who had moved, could not present his paper. In fact, he was expelled—officially this time—from the IPA, and the conditions of this expulsion were particularly perverse. In his hagiography of Freud,

Jones says Reich resigned from the IPA. Nothing could be further from the truth. When Reich arrived in Lucerne under difficult conditions (he had run out of money), he knew nothing of his expulsion from the Berlin society. He only discovered this when he noticed that he was not listed in the IPA brochure. Thinking that this was the work of the Aryan duo (Boehm and Müller-Braunschweig), he turned to Anna Freud, assuming she would help him. But Anna Freud and Jones then countered him with a purely technical argument: As long as he was not a member of a local organization, he could not be a member of the International Association. Yet Jones had led an intense underhanded campaign against Reich and was personally assured that no one would welcome him.[32] His expulsion was a strong signal: Fearing his fate, the entire Freudian left—despite being in the majority—gave up.[33]

Faced with the obvious internal decay of psychoanalysis and the failure of its political achievements (the crushing of the Communist Party in 1933 suspended Reich's attempts with the Sexpol), Otto Fenichel decided, from 1934 onwards, to distribute clandestine pamphlets in order to maintain a left analytic tradition:[34] "We were convinced that we saw in Freud's psychoanalysis the seed of a future dialectical-materialist psychoanalysis, which is why we desperately needed to protect and spread this knowledge."[35] On the other hand, following the congress, Anna Freud thanked Jones for not having mixed up psychoanalysis with political activity.

However, the attempt by Jones and his Aryan acolytes to adapt psychoanalysis to the Third Reich remained incomplete. On October 24, 1935, Edith Jacobson, an analyst trained in Berlin and analyzed by Otto Fenichel, was arrested by the Gestapo and accused of a plot against the state and high treason. She had authorized members of a social democrat group, to which one of her patients belonged, to hold a meeting at her home. Faced with this situation, the proponents of the new "rescue" direction were quick to put forth new requirements. A hasty meeting of the German Psychoanalytic Society was held on November 30, 1935, with Jones in attendance. Rather than shutting down the society and calling for resistance by organizing for the withdrawal of German analysts and their repatriation to areas where the practice of free psychoanalysis was still possible, a new rule was imposed on all members that extended the principle of "political neutrality": Analysts were prohibited from taking on a politically engaged patient for treatment. This rule, in practice impossible to maintain, caused deep rifts among analysts. During this meeting, for which we have two accounts,[36] Boehm kept insisting on the fact that psychoanalysis was not a *Weltanschauung*. Again, in the name of this argument, some members wondered about the relevance of withdrawing from the IPA, which remained marked by Freud's name and his Jewishness. According to Bernd Nitzschke, Boehm, Müller-Braunschweig, and the majority of the Aryan members of the committee, including Jones, ultimately "advised" Jewish members of the German Psychoanalytic Society to resign. Jones rejected all propositions by psychoanalysts like Rollenbleck and Herold, which suggested dissolving the society and continuing to practice illegally. Only one non-Jew, Bernhard Kamm, resigned in solidarity.

The departure of many members opened up opportunities for others. Kemper, an Aryan psychoanalyst, soon took on responsibilities in the German Society, becoming its third president, alongside Boehm and Müller-Braunschweig. For his part, Müller-Braunschweig continued his campaign for the "modernization of psychoanalysis": Praising National Socialism, he declared in "Psychoanalysis and Germanness" that it was now possible to give the Psychoanalytic Society "a truly German face," which was not the case in the past given the "international" origins of its members.

However, German Psychoanalytic Society members were not at ease. Worried they were not giving the Nazi regime enough guarantees in the wake of the "Jacobson episode," they finally felt it more "prudent" to leave their parent organization, the IPA, in order to "rescue" the society, and decided to submit a resignation request for it. An unnecessary precaution, since the promotion of the "rescue strategy" and "neutral psychoanalysis" was soon crowned with success. In 1936, the German Psychoanalytic Society became attached to the German Institute for Psychological Research and Psychotherapy, led by Matthias Göring, a cousin of the marshal [Hermann Göring], who was "sympathetic" to psychoanalysis. After the "voluntary resignation" of the Jewish members, nothing stood in the way of this affiliation. Thus, "liberated from Jews" and the "Reds," and sworn to Hitler, the German Psychoanalytic Society withdrew its request to leave the IPA and remained a member until 1938.

This was too much for some politically engaged analysts: John Rittmeister, a psychoanalyst and militant revolutionary socialist, opposed the transformation of the Berlin policlinic in vain. While continuing to practice there, he joined the resistance secretly, where he hosted meetings connected to the powerful Red Orchestra network.[37] For his part, Müller-Braunschweig, now the society's treasurer, did not hesitate to demand the Jewish members forced into exile repay their training debts. When the payments did not come, he complained to Jones, who helped him to collect them.

Together with Felix Boehm and Carl Müller-Braunschweig, Herbert Linden, an official member of the Nazi Party who would later be heavily involved in the Nazis' extermination program, first proposed the idea of a German Institute of Psychotherapy to Matthias Göring. The aim was to create an organization available to all the branches of psychotherapy.[38] Jones publicly defended the affiliation of the German Psychoanalytic Institute with the Göring Institute, particularly at the Marienbad congress during the summer of 1936. For Jones, this affiliation was the "guarantee for psychoanalysis" to "maintain its independence."[39] Both Freud and his daughter "thought that Boehm would be doing psychoanalysis a favor by creating this Society."[40] After the Berlin policlinic, the German Institute would soon "absorb" the Vienna one.

In 1938, Austria was invaded by the German army. Fenichel commented on the attitude of his Viennese colleagues who, facing the Nazis' entrance the city, acted like "usual Viennese Burghers: a short agitated panic followed by a great confidence in the present government."[41] Pursuing his politics of Aryanization, Carl Müller-Braunschweig planned to establish the *German Journal of*

Psychoanalysis on Third Reich Soil. He also sought non-Jewish and German analysts to achieve this merger. He wrote to Sterba, an early Viennese analyst trained by Reich:

> I would like to inform you briefly about the local events. After the resignation (!) of the Jewish members, the Vienna Psychoanalytic Society has been absorbed by the German Psychoanalytic Society. The next task is to construct out of Berggasse 7 an institute that, like the one in Berlin, permits the different psychotherapeutic schools to work on a basis of equality ... For this we urgently need the full cooperation and assistance of the few Aryan members of the Vienna Psychoanalytic Society ... As a member of the German Psychoanalytic Society, you will—if there are no special reasons against this—without further ado, become a member also of the German Institute and in this way would be recognized as a psychotherapist in Germany. With collegial greetings and HEIL HITLER! Yours, Carl Müller-Braunschweig.[42]

Sterba declined the offer and decided to emigrate to England with his whole family. There, he wrote to Jones to ask for help. The latter's reply was scathing: "you should have stayed in Vienna together with August Aichhorn as a memory of psychoanalysis for a happier future.[43]" Sterba, who had the audacity to oppose the "rescue" project, would have to fend for himself.

Until 1938, the Göring Institute was affiliated with the IPA without provoking any reaction. At the Paris Congress in 1938, Jones maintained that the German

Psychoanalytic Society enjoyed "substantial independence." But that same year, Göring secured its dissolution, and it was only then that its representation at the IPA also ended. The members of the old Psychoanalytic Society were from then on integrated into the institute's "section A."

This black page that saw, thanks to the IPA's active support, the collapse of German psychoanalysis *in* and *with* Nazism, would leave its mark on the entire international psychoanalytic movement. Its principal architect, Jones, would remain president of the IPA during and after the war. In the postwar period, although the English psychoanalyst John Rickman recommended that none of the analysts active in the institutions during the Nazi period should be entrusted with a position in a psychoanalytic organization, Jones didn't see it that way. In a 1949 speech, he did not hesitate to defend the idea that Müller-Braunschweig was one of the few under Hitler who had remained "real, true analysts."[44] Indeed, he entrusted him with the task of creating a new psychoanalytic group, the German Psychoanalytic Association, which was formed in 1950. Müller-Braunschweig had meanwhile resigned from his presidency in the former German Psychoanalytic Society, reconstituted after the German defeat, but which, given its recent past, could hardly be affiliated again with the IPA. Boehm would take over. As Nitzschke wrote, two analytic societies coexisted in Germany, both claiming to have contributed to the "rescue of psychoanalysis."

The influence of a revolutionary psychoanalytic practice would not be felt in Germany and Austria for a long time.⁴⁵ Despite all of Aichhorn's efforts after the war, it was only in 1999 that Ambulatorium, the free policlinic in Vienna, resumed its activities.⁴⁶ For the time being, the energy of political psychoanalysis would take other paths.

4
Marie Langer: From 1930s Vienna to 1970s Latin America

Marie Langer's Resistance in 1930s Vienna

A far cry from Ernest Jones's maneuvers in Germany, Marie Langer's career shows the possibility of taking a completely different path. Her story begins in Vienna in 1935. Marie Langer was twenty-five and went to Vienna to finish her medical studies. Austrian fascism was in power in the country, and for many of her contemporaries, the situation seemed desperate. But Langer believed in the persistence and vitality of the emancipatory movements—particularly feminist and communist—to which she belonged. These acted underground to keep the legacy of the 1920s alive:

> In the socialists' Red Vienna, there was a solid tradition of feminist struggle; from the start, the Social-Democrats supported the belief that women should be able to decide the fate of their own bodies, which resulted in the struggle to legalize abortion, against Article 144, which condemned it. This struggle was fought by the proletarian women's branch of the Socialist Party, and from there, towards communism.[1]

As we have seen, Stalin's paternalistic hegemony had not yet wreaked its havoc on the Austrian Communist Party. During these years, for many communists, revolutionary militancy included the fight for equality of the sexes. Alongside her work as a psychoanalyst, Langer secretly practiced anesthesia with her friend, the gynecologist Fritz Jensen, also a member of the Communist party; they helped to perform abortions on women who, due to economic or political reasons, could not get them under good conditions. In the 1930s, during which time paternalism and fascist antisemitism had gained considerable ground and dominated the political scene, Red Vienna was not yet dead. With other resistance fighters, Langer kept the flame alive. The February Revolution of 1917, started by women and largely driven by turn-of-the-century feminism, provided Langer with a sure compass during these reactionary times.

Like Reich, the Marxist-feminist psychoanalyst Marie Langer embodies the people's history of psychoanalysis in her career and her stances. Generally "absent" from official history, her trajectory sheds light on one of the most fertile periods of twentieth-century psychoanalysis, fraught with issues and conflicts that have marked the history of the discipline—and she reported on this many times during her life. The fact that her clinical-political works and her historical testimony of psychoanalysis and of her revolutionary commitment remain untranslated into French [or English] raises the question about the "forgetting" that still marks her career. If the figure of Reich remains emblematic of the period from the beginning of the 1920s to the beginning of the 1930s, Marie Langer's—

who to our knowledge never met him—provides a red thread running through the entire history of psychoanalysis. Her words, her concerns, and the choices she made in face of historical necessities reveal many aspects of the discipline's revolutionary side, cleverly obscured by the orthodoxy.

Early Years

Marie Langer was born in Vienna, in 1910, under Emperor Franz Josef's reign. Her childhood, adolescence, and youth occurred during intense political upheavals. With a touch of humor, she would later characterize her relation to history as an "imperial Oedipus complex."[2] World War I marked a break for her: Her father had to join the front line when she was only four years old. At that point, which perhaps decided her orientation towards care, she wanted to become a nurse, since nurses were the only women allowed to go to war—and as she stressed, it was the way for her, still a small girl, to stay close to her father. The death of Emperor Franz Josef in 1916 was a new socio-historic entry in her Oedipus complex. At just seven years old, she saw it as nothing less than the "death of God." The world collapsed for the social class to which she belonged: For this Jewish family in the haute bourgeoisie, though educated and atheist, the emperor's reign seemed truly immutable, and his person "immortal." It was impossible to envision a reversal of the existing order.

The irruption of history into the closed world of the conservative bourgeoisie would push Langer to emancipate herself, first and foremost from the "resigned" model embodied by her mother, whom Langer described as frigid. From Langer's reading of Schopenhauer, her mother seemed to prove the German philosopher's misogyny: She was the "proper Mother-wife" who could have been "a typical patient of Freud's."[3] Despite the relative cultural liberation[4] that her family experienced after the war (the day after the armistice, the republic was proclaimed), her mother continued like "Madame Bovary" to dream of a true love, the very thing that keeps women under masculine domination and that Alexandra Kollontaï denounced. But Langer didn't mistake her enemy. If at this point she was critical of her mother, it was because she saw her as the product of "a social situation that seemed permanent." And so "her feminist claims for women were also a way of reclaiming her mother's repressed femininity."[5]

With her father's support, Marie Langer began her studies. She enrolled at the Schwarzwald Schule, whose director, Frau Doktor Schwarzwald, was a socialist with liberal morals. She went on to study in Zurich at the first university open to women—it was impossible at that time for women to pursue higher education in Austria—where future Russian revolutionaries were also educated. The majority of her professors "were Marxists and very politically involved," and the school held to a "feminist and Marxist line."[6] According to her own account, Marie Langer received crucial training there. She went on to study medicine and received her degree in 1935.

During this time, antisemitism was gaining momentum. At the university, Langer witnessed targeted attacks against Jewish students, which took place under the eyes of the police, who did nothing to prevent it. After attending a Hitler rally, she decided to join the underground Communist Party. The revolutionary perspective took hold of her. Political engagement also allowed her to combine two struggles: against the violent social destiny of women and against the fate of the Jews. Having been born into a bourgeois family under the emperor's reign had not protected her from this twofold mission: "Even though we were rich, I was aware of my two disadvantages: being Jewish and being a woman. Later a third was added: being divorced. For this reason, joining the left seemed the only logical solution: I was certain that communism would abolish this marginalization."[7]

Medicine was largely "socialized" then and freshly graduated students had to practice for two years at the

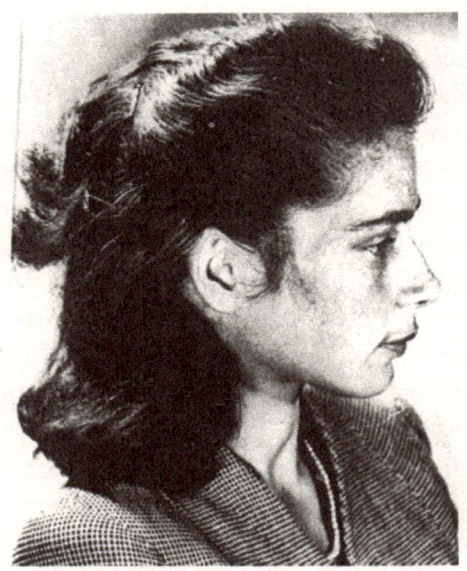

Figure 4   Maria Langer

hospital, trying out various specialties. Langer opted for psychiatry and began analysis with Richard Sterba, the first salaried employee of the Vienna Psychoanalytic Society (Wiener Psychoanalytische Vereinigung). But in a country now in fascist hands, where antisemitism became official policy, non-Catholic doctors were gradually excluded from positions in the institution. Langer therefore chose to undergo "didactic" psychoanalytic training to become an analyst. This is how she met Anna Freud, and in the early 1930s she joined the Vienna Psychoanalytic Society, where some enthusiasm still reigned. Despite Freud's reversal being underway—which was perhaps not yet clear to everyone—it went without saying for Langer and the other Viennese analysts that psychoanalysis had its place in society: "In Vienna, everyone agreed that psychoanalysis should be applied to the school system and to education, as well as in drafting legislation and reforming the prison system."[8] Within the institution, she pursued her training and read the whole of Freud's work, without abandoning her political militancy. In that period, for young analysts training in Vienna, there was no disconnect between Freud and Marx.

Impossible Neutrality

After being arrested for belonging to a group of doctors working to promote peace (which also included her future second husband, Max Langer), Marie Langer was forced by the previous generation of Viennese analysts to make an impossible choice between psychoanalysis and militancy. Edward Bibring, an eminent member of the Vienna Psychoanalytic Society, had learned of her misadventure from one of his analysands, who was also Langer's colleague and friend. Outraged by Marie Langer's activism—and without regard for the secrecy of the analyst's couch—he suggested to his colleagues in the society that she be expelled. Thanks to Sterba's intervention, Marie Langer narrowly escaped this sanction, but she was nonetheless admonished by the society's president, Paul Federn.[9]

In reality, the new rule of "political abstinence" turned out in practice to be very far from the prescribed so-called neutrality. It plunged all of the analytic society's members into serious conflicts and irresolvable contradictions. Federn himself, who in this episode played the role of the authoritarian father, was known for his socialism, and one of his sons was threatened for belonging to Trotskyist circles—arrested by the Gestapo in 1938, he would be deported to Buchenwald. In addition to the young generation, most of the society's leading members also faced an impossible choice, all the more for having been the main figures in Freudian psychoanalysis since the 1920s; they had built its institutions and the discipline had gained an unprecedented position in most European capitals, east and west, precisely due to their political commitment to social progress. As a result, Freud's "retreat," both his theoretical pessimism and this new "pragmatics" that called for "adapting" psychoanalysis in order to "rescue it," proved impractical for them.

Langer's testimony is invaluable here. The analysts in the Vienna Psychoanalytic Society were not only prohibited to engage in political activity that had become illegal—all the opposition parties were now forbidden—but, more seriously, they were also banned from undertaking or continuing treatment with politically engaged patients. Langer highlighted the "ethical" but also "ideological conflict" that resulted from challenging the rules of treatment. Many analysts were in fact treating seriously ill patients for whom it was impossible to stop treatment for obvious reasons. For the patients, prevented from speaking about their political activities, the rule of free association had been broken.[10] The psychoanalyst thus had only three possibilities, all which were dead ends for Langer: "interrupt treatment, forbid the patient's political activity, or accept, in an unspoken alliance, that the patient continues their activity, without talking too much about it."[11]

Following her arrest and the incident with Bibring, Langer was afraid. A genuine paranoia had justifiably taken over the country. The secret police had infiltrated everywhere, including analytic circles, and even more in the militant circles that Langer continued to frequent and even organize. It was known that shortly beforehand in Germany, Edith Jacobson had been arrested by the Gestapo under suspicion of collaborating with the Social Democrats. It was pointed out that this highly significant fact should have led to the dissolution of all psychoanalytic activity in the country, but paradoxically it convinced Jones (with Freud's blessing) to impose the misnamed rule of "political abstinence" on the clinic itself. Marie Langer commented on the general orientation towards "rescue," with the neutrality measure imposed on analysts being only one aspect: "To save the values of psychoanalysis, these same values were attacked in their very essence."[12]

This unresolvable contradiction would sweep away most of the great Freudians in its whirlwind. Faced with what Langer called Freud's "political myopia," the leading figures took their stand: Some, like Jones, assumed this policy and saw it through it to its end, while others unambiguously disassociated themselves from it.

As for Marie Langer, she did not attend Freud's eightieth birthday and, agreeing with Sterba to stop her analysis, she and her husband decided to join the International Brigades in Spain during the summer of 1936.[13] Confronted with a threat of civilizational collapse into fascist darkness, she decried it would be "absurd to surrender without a fight": "we couldn't be navel-gazing while the world burned."[14] With a police record, she had little choice anyway if she wanted to continue the fight. Her daughter Veronica reported her mother's observations on this period: "the left saved my life. Without the left, I would have stayed in Vienna, and I would have been killed as a Jew."[15]

The International Brigades in Spain

Marie Langer's arrival in Spain was a joyful experience: "Nowhere before or since have I seen a city so gay, so full of music and enthusiasm, and as happy as Barcelona was then. [...] La Rambla looked like a party."[16] The people were celebrating their victory; all the residents were mobilized in a kind of revolutionary fervor. Langer's descriptions match with those of Orwell, who recalled streets where red and black flags flew, and emphasized the enthusiastic commitment of a liberated population, proud to have its dignity back. François Tosquelles, a Catalan psychoanalyst and an active player in the revolution within the POUM (Worker's Party of Marxist Unification)—to whom we will return in the next chapter—also noted the similarity between Barcelona in this time and Red Vienna at the height of its revolutionary ferment.

In Catalonia, Langer's political engagement found new inspiration. As a woman, she felt she totally belonged. She found that "the Spanish left indeed gave a prominent place to women," who "were involved in decision-making." She met Dolores Ibárruri, the *Pasionaria* [the passionate one], "the highest female authority in the Spanish communist party," as well as Federica Montseny, a very important figure among the anarchists.[17] At the front line in Aragon, Langer was fascinated by the political climate. The territory was then held by the anarchists. When she visited the villages, she found the same enthusiasm, the same happiness, and the same generosity as in Barcelona, so much that the experience seemed "unreal" to her. The reigning political euphoria, the experience of equality between men and women, the abolition of capitalism put into practice to an unprecedented degree, and the possibility of expressing political convictions without hiding marked her for life. During these guerilla years with her husband and other colleagues, she learned a great deal about war surgery. Her small group performed grueling operations on those wounded at the front. At the Murcia hospital where she practiced, the atmosphere was internationalist: There were "two North American surgeons, father and son, the Dutch head nurse, the Bulgarian hospital director, and many others."[18] And the Brigades spoke in French.

Lacking means to make suitable prosthetics for the amputees, she and her husband attempted to raise money in Paris to purchase the orthopedic equipment that was in seriously short supply. But for the Spaniards who secretly crossed the Pyrenees, finding money was no easy task, especially since the situation in Spain seemed hopeless from the French perspective. Both the French and English Popular Front kept to the "non-intervention" pact. While they awaited news from their contact in Paris, the couple took shelter in Nice, where Marie Langer went through the worst period of her life: She lost a child there, a little girl born prematurely, and sunk into depression. In 1938, surprised by the Anschluss that obliterated any possibility of returning to Vienna and pushed Europe to the brink of war, the couple went into exile: first in Uruguay, then in Argentina in 1942. There Langer finally found asylum and returned to psychoanalysis: In 1942 she took part in the founding of the Argentinian Psychoanalytic Association (APA), affiliated with the IPA, headed by Jones—but it was at the price of muting her militancy.

The Need for Self-Censorship in the Psychoanalytic Association

Upon arriving in Argentina, Langer had to remake her life, and she had everything to prove. The political situation was not good. Between 1946 and 1955, with Juan Perón in power, far left militancy was impossible. It was therefore best to stay "calm and still, so that the young APA was not put at risk." Scalded by her experience with the Vienna Psychoanalytic Society, Langer thus forced herself to separate her activity as an analyst from her ties with the left: "For several decades," she centered her "devotion" and her "loyalty not on politics but to an institutional-analytic 'militancy.'"[19] She invested herself in the APA and wrote extensively, including *Maternity and Sex*. This book, in a process of continual revisions and edits, bore the scars of the compromises resulting from her break with political activity. In it, Langer was led to adapt, or even betray, her convictions. Between the first and second editions, for example, her publisher asked her to remove passages that established a Marxist perspective, which she confided that she accepted by "self-censoring." This very particular context also explains her theoretical bias towards a certain "biologizing Kleinianism" that consisted in naturalizing the place of women. Indeed, Langer acknowledged that Freudian phallocentrism did not satisfy her and prevented her from "meeting her patients"; if not feminist or revolutionary, Klein's perspective at least seemed to assert the specificity of feminine psychology.[20] Moreover, the APA as a whole was Kleinian in orientation, which was not without its dogmatic consequences.[21] Exile, and the precarity it breeds, made Langer particularly dependent on the association. A woman, immigrant, and mother of four children, she "had to keep quiet" in order to survive:

I arrived in Argentina with a precarious training and practically broke. Until I could get my diploma validated again, which happened well after I arrived in Buenos Aires, I had to keep silent on several occasions. [...] One day, I would love to talk about the consequences of exile, I was a second-class citizen.[22]

By her own admission, she sometimes made regressive interpretations of her patients, women patients in particular. Referencing, Freud's text, Langer described the reigning ideology as a *Weltanschaaung* (worldview) typical of analytic institutions. She thus tried to trade her political militancy for a purely analytic militancy. Until, having regained social stability, she could gradually reconnect with her "fighting spirit."

Political Reawakening

A first milestone in Marie Langer's return to a clinic-political articulation is in her book *Group Psychotherapy*, co-written in 1956 with two other psychoanalysts and doctors, Emilio Rodrigué and Léon Grinberg. From a consideration of countertransference as a decisive therapeutic tool, the authors orient Kleinianism towards group therapy; this enabled psychoanalysis to be applied to underprivileged classes, particularly in hospitals, in keeping with Freud's wish for a psychoanalysis accessible to as many people as possible. But Langer waited for more than a decade to disavow openly the prejudices she herself had put forward in the name of the supposed neutrality of psychoanalysis and its clinical practice in order to be recognized as a full member of the IPA. Once again, historical events drove her to take up this courageous self-critique. In the heart of the 1960s, she found the still smoldering embers of her Spanish experience, which she confided to her daughter Veronica was her "lost paradise,"[23] and she was able to reconnect with her original political commitment.

In 1966, as part of the fight against the Vietnam War, her daughter invited her to participate in a commemoration of the struggle of the International Brigades in Spain. Langer describes: "I thought it was the return, that I was going back to the place I had left. I thought about it all night. The next day I accepted. [...] This decision marked the beginning of my return to politics."[24] Summoned by her own past like Antigone, she would no longer give up on her desire. Here the self-critique that she takes up in her books *Group Psychotherapy* and *Maternity and Sex* becomes clear. First, she disavowed the naïve perspective that the "healing" that analysis aims for was not affected by the analyst's ideology (we will come back to this). Second, after her trip to Cuba in 1973, she admitted to having succumbed to the "idealization of motherhood." Taking on the pertinent critique addressed to her by the psychoanalyst Juliet Mitchell, she acknowledged her old prejudices: "I was—like other psychoanalysts—persuaded [...] of the fundamental importance of a mother–child relationship for the mental health of both. But [...] is it so damaging that in the socialist countries many children are raised from their second week of life in nurseries? I don't think so."[25] She believed that she then had to "pay for feminine pleasure with motherhood." This lucid self-critique cannot be understood outside the situation in Buenos Aires at the end of the 1960s, and its developments, which were reminiscent of 1920s Vienna or Barcelona in 1936.

In Argentina, the new postwar generation of analysts, psychiatrists, and psychologists had been trained in Marxism. A great number of them worked in psychiatry and wanted to transform the structure of asylums.

The Argentinian Federation of Psychiatry (FAP), whose eventual president Emilio Rodrigué was also a prominent analyst in the APA, was also moving in this direction. After the military coup in 1966, analysts were pushed to take a stand. The APA itself seemed to support the social protest movement: It made an official statement in favor of the youth movements and rebellion, warning against the state and ongoing repression.[26] Many of its influential members (including Langer) were probably behind this statement: There was no question of them repeating the choice that was imposed on analysts in the IPA in the 1930s. It was not true that the analyst could be neutral, especially in such a climate!

During the same period, an international movement of analysts that had developed in Switzerland and in Italy initiated a critique of the IPA, both of its top-down modes of training and organization and its bourgeois and conservative ideology. As reported by Armando Bauléo, the association's Argentinian representative, it was Berthold Rothschild, a member of the Zurich psychoanalytic seminar, and Elvio Fachinelli, from the Gruppo Milanese per lo sviluppo della psicoterapia, who launched the movement during the IPA's Rome Congress. Dubbed Plataforma internacional, it would soon bring together analysts of sixteen nationalities.[27] The escalating violence and state terror in Argentina, which in 1969 led to the repression of the Cordobazo, a popular uprising that brought together workers and students, would precipitate things: The political tendency within the APA, to which Langer belonged, was affiliated with Plataforma, which allowed its members to politicize the association openly. Naturally, the APA leadership reacted quite negatively to these demonstrations of political engagement, recalling the "necessary neutrality of psychoanalysis."[28] The split was finally effected in 1971, when the leadership refused to publish the text of the speech Langer delivered in Vienna that same year, where she asserted that she would renounce neither Marx nor Freud. The political tendency collectively resigned from the APA, and then from the IPA.

But while the murderous repression of the Cordobazo was reminiscent of the repression of the revolt in Vienna in 1927 and its denunciation by Reich,[29] followed by his expulsion, this split had diametrically opposed effects in Argentina. First, the APA not only saw a significant part of its membership quit the association—including the most brilliant members—but it also lost its monopoly on analytic training. Next, this jolt led to profound changes in its organization: the admission of full members to the rank of teaching specialist on request, the right of associate members to vote in the assemblies, opening to non-medical psychologists, etc. Last but not least, it marked the birth of a new politically engaged analytic current with the workers—in particular through the Teaching and Research Centers (Centros de Docencia e Investigacion, or CDI)[30]—under the name Plataforma Argentina.[31] This political split also found an important echo in civil society and the intellectual world. The magazine *Los Libros* remarked with foresight: "the conflict that shook the Argentinian psychoanalytic institution in recent months appears to be indicative of a global situation that concerns us all, insofar as the problems it reveals are tied to the future of the culture, i.e. the political future of the whole country."[32]

Plataforma Argentina and New Psychoanalytic Praxis

Plataforma Argentina's dissident current allowed for an open challenge to the class ideology hidden behind the supposed neutrality of the analytic institution and the hypocrisy of its privileges—including the monopoly on analyst status by doctors alone. Its foundational letter, whose final drafting fell to Emilio Rodrigué, made no secret that it was finally assuming a political orientation. It was addressed directly to the "healthcare workers" with whom the psychoanalysts signing-on identified. From the outset, it asserted the resolutely secular nature of psychoanalysis, as well as its necessary involvement in society—real taboos for the APA and its *establishment* [in English]:

> We, the undersigned psychoanalysts constituting the group Plataforma Argentina, which incorporates the movement Plataforma internacional, hereby publicly resolve to separate from the International Psychoanalytic Association and its Argentinian subsidiary. [...] We know that this choice transcends us as psychoanalysts and as individuals, and takes on a much broader meaning beyond the context of scientific and institutional life. To explain the motivations and proposals driving us, we address ourselves to mental healthcare workers, including ourselves as their colleagues. With this declaration [...] we aim to give all sectors a clear picture of our identity.[33]

The letter continues with a radical critique of the analytic organization, which in many respects remains a burning issue. Its ideology, supposedly developed in "defense" of psychoanalysis, ended up "paralyzing" and "sterilizing" it from a scientific perspective. It allowed unnatural "pacts" between "science and the ideological system of the ruling class," which have marked the APA, where many aspiring analysts remain at the bottom of the ladder "without being able to participate in the organization." Like capitalist society, the institution is built on economic privileges and the domination of the few "at the top of the pyramid." The consequence is that the analysts "locked themselves up" in the school and "cut themselves off from social reality," resulting in "a form of sheltering of the figure of the analyst." From there, they can lay claim, at least in imagination, to an "apolitical and asocial professional activity": Their dominant social position is rationalized by the criterion of "neutrality of value judgements." As the alleged scientific guarantee of analysis, neutrality instead participates in a "utopian" political-historical vision, where "all social transformation is supposed to be an illusion," against which the "ethics of psychoanalysis," like its "professionalism," can serve as a bulwark.[34]

In a time of dictatorship, the false pretenses of the bourgeoisie that made up the institution were no longer tenable for the critics in Plataforma. The political moment demanded that, in order to survive without betraying its path, psychoanalysis had to break with an institution that was corrupt at every level. It must join the popular struggle and participate in revolutionary transformative work:

We are in the process of becoming and forming other psychoanalysts, bringing together all who wish to collaborate in this direction. We want to practice true psychoanalysis. This decision commits us to our work and denounces it at the same time: we join other scientists and professionals who understand that their science cannot and must not build a wall that isolates and distances it from social reality or from its own theoretical tool, thereby transforming it into a mystifying and mystified tool working against change. From this day on, psychoanalysis is no longer for us the official psychoanalytic institution. Psychoanalysis will be where psychoanalysts are [...] no longer an isolated and isolating scientific field, but a science involved in the multiple realities that it claims to study and transform.[35]

Eduardo Pavlovsky and Gregorio Baremblitt, psychoanalysts involved in the movement, described the dissidents' fertile state of mind and commitment:

We took over every available space. [...] We politicized the struggle of the association by overcoming discrimination and the absurd old prejudices among psychiatrists, psychologists, and educational psychologists. [...] The coordination of mental healthcare workers and the teaching and research center where we met offered, for a modest fee, psychoanalytic training for all, from a new Marxist angle. During the dictatorship, we struggled alongside the Forum for Human Rights, the Commission of Relatives of Political Prisoners, Students, and Trade Unions (COFAPPEG) and the Lawyer's Union against torture of prisoners and for their liberation. We joined the worker's struggle. We participated in its demonstrations. [...] Everyone took part [...] in the struggle to end the dictatorship, with the aim of free elections and the establishment of a popular anti-imperialist government.[36]

While the APA would meet a dubious fate that recalled the Berlin policlinic's disastrous "rescue of psychoanalysis" and the "adaptation" to Nazism, the new revolutionary direction given by Plataforma to psychoanalysis proved to be full of lessons. Langer attests to this: "We made a number of concrete advances in the much-debated field of the reciprocal relationship between Marxism and psychoanalysis, by granting practice the importance Marx, Gramsci, and Mao accorded it." In particular, she mentions her clinical experience in the hospital of Avellaneda in 1970, where "a valuable praxis that integrated Marxism and psychoanalysis in practice" was partly successful. For Langer and her psychoanalyst comrades, the aim was to reintroduce the social reality of class into the evaluation of the treatment. In their own way, they were reconnecting with the analysts of the 1920s.

The New Psychoanalytic Clinic in Avellaneda

In fact, Langer's concept of treatment recalls certain aspects of the analytic technique Reich elaborated in the 1920s. Like him, Langer observed that among the working classes, psychic affliction was closely linked to social condition, with which it tended to merge. And like Reich, her clinic led her to observe that poor women suffered disproportionately. She also drew the conclusion—which is the first basic technical requirement of this approach—that to practice analysis one must consider the patient's "socio-economic-cultural situation": "for example, you cannot demand that a housewife abandon her home, spend money on transportation, rely on a neighbor to take care of the children, and ask her husband to prepare meals too often." Starting from the same premises as Reich, Langer still developed an original treatment technique.

Revisiting her experience in Avellaneda, she explains:

> Certainly, when faced with a working-class male patient, I would say that along with the consciousness of his psychic conflict, he must also acquire class consciousness. And this did not mean, as a mental health goal, to work better or more for his boss, but instead for his own interests, for example, the union. And what was said for the male worker also applies to the woman: beyond her class belonging she should become aware of her submission to the man, her excessive dependence on love, an expression of lack of self-esteem, and an important goal of her analysis would be to gain dignity. In general terms, I would add to the concept of treatment (from classical psychoanalysis) what Freud suggests when he talks about the need to transform an autoplastic attitude into an alloplastic one [...] This implies a dialectical game with oneself, in which the subject can adapt reality to its needs but also know how to adapt to it. This can be compared to Marx's formula that we are in the world in order to transform it.[37]

As with Reich, her aim was to articulate analysis on two levels, psychic and social, and to bring to light their entanglement in order to enable the subject to emerge from their subjective and material impasse by transforming it. But whereas Reich engaged in far-reaching preventative action and politicized the sexual question, Langer sought to redefine both the objective and the form of treatment.

In the first place, the treatment's success must be judged in terms of the subject's real transformation, which also entails the improvement of their social condition. On this point, Langer partly agrees with Reich in critiquing a technical approach limited to improving symptoms. For her, the analyst must go further in the treatment by working to diminish the feelings of guilt that contribute to maintaining the patient in their condition:

> Aside from improving symptoms, our goal was to help our patients lose or at least diminish their sexual and social prejudices and to free themselves relatively from the ideology of the ruling class. It was also to achieve sudden discoveries by weakening repression and unconscious feelings of guilt. These often originated from their belief that they were the only ones responsible for their own failures. We tried to help them distinguish between their own responsibility, their family's and society's, according to their own history. We claimed that they could acquire a different consciousness and vision of themselves and the world, understand how they were conditioned to occupy the place that society assigned to them, and make decisions that could offer

a way out of their situation (many began their studies, others to take active interest in social processes).[38]

In other words, elaborating the individual history through the transference must go hand-in-hand with the subject's consciousness of the social determinants that have structured it, but also with the singular elaboration that gives them the means to transform their destiny of domination. Here, analytic healing acquires a materialist dimension.

To achieve this new objective, Langer questioned the classical form of treatment. In fact, the proletarian subject suffering from neurosis had a more complicated treatment path due to their class situation. For the analyst, it was not simply helping develop *insight* [English]—an ability to interpret their inner world—nor bringing them to sharpen their consciousness of the oppression they suffer. In any case, such objectives are only truly attainable if and only if the analyst can contribute at the same time to the concrete transformation of the patient's isolated social condition. This is why Langer and her colleagues decided to "collectivize" treatment, so to speak, by organizing group sessions. These would have a key function in creating a new social bond capable of bringing about the intended changes:

> But for this to happen, and for the person who needs therapeutic help at some point to be able to continue on their own without therapy, they need to acquire not only an *insight* into the psychological problems that have led to their illness but also the necessary tools to

understand how society and the place they occupy in it condition their own lives. And this awareness would not be operational either unless it simultaneously manages to break out of its isolation and to forge bonds of solidarity beyond its own private world. This process was particularly important for working-class housewives, who made up about a third of our patients and who often lived in total isolation. We were able to see how the therapeutic process of the groups evolved as solidarity between group participants emerged and consolidated, despite existing rivalries, tensions, and ambivalence. In the groups, we countered the system's pathogenic competition with solidarity.[39]

For Langer, an effective treatment could not be individual: The discoordination between the social space where classic treatment unfolds and the patient's ordinary everyday life is such that it risks preventing any therapeutic process. It is necessary but not sufficient only to take into account the ordinary vicissitudes in which the patient is caught—think of the housewife who cannot leave her house. The treatment must also be transformed so it can bring about a modification in the social relations in a better direction for the patient. Group treatment is an immediate first tool for this change. It organizes the experience of a solidarity between its members that breaks with ordinary competition, offering the subject another subjective and collective basis for finding the means to change their social conditions.

The Shutdown by the Dictatorship and the "Neutrality" of Psychoanalysis

In 1974, Marie Langer was suddenly forced to stop her work and return to exile after she published a letter denouncing the actions of Amilcar Lobo Moreira, a Brazilian analyst who participated in torture under his country's dictatorship.[40] Ironically, he had been trained in the Brazilian psychoanalysis school whose founder, Kemper, was a former member of the Göring Institute. "Adapting" psychoanalysis to the worst regimes thus continued over time and across borders. Imported to Brazil by Kemper, the 1930s template would soon be revived and regain its fatal power in Argentina. Marie Langer was once again caught up in history.

Shortly after the publication of this letter, she was warned by one of her analysands that her name was on the "Triple A" list established by the Argentinian Anticommunist Alliance's death squads. Her life was in danger. Since 1973, paramilitary groups directed by the "Minister of Social Welfare" were seeking to eliminate all political opposition. Some analysts were arrested during session under their patients' eyes. Others were kidnapped or imprisoned for treating opponents. In this tragic period in Latin American history, the institution of psychoanalism, once again under the banner of "neutrality," distinguished itself by its marked compromise with the worst powers: The IPA covered up Moreira—endangering the life of Langer's colleague who warned her[41]—while the APA continued its activities as if nothing happened under the dictatorship, even receiving financial support from the military. The paternalist, familialist version of psychoanalism defended by the APA provided the generals with precious ideological backing to support their propaganda of rebuilding society on "healthy values." The very people who claimed to be its proponents, in contradiction, provided new tragic proof of the impossibility of a politically neutral psychoanalysis.

But if the institution of psychoanalism persisted in deadly denial of its own relation to history—stammering about the "adaptive" direction of the 1930s—Marie Langer, like many others, would pursue her revolutionary clinical and political commitment until the end of her life, from Nicaragua (particularly with the Sandinistas) to Cuba. History was not just repeating itself: This time, a whole generation of analysts had been able through their actions to assume and demonstrate openly and collectively—sometimes risking their lives—what was at stake in the fight for a people's psychoanalysis. In going beyond revisionism and reconnecting with the politicized perspective of the Freudians of the 1920s, the path of true psychoanalysis had been rediscovered in Latin America.

5
From the Catalonian Commune to La Borde Clinic

Tosquelles and the 1930s in Catalonia

In 1931, as the landscape darkened elsewhere in Europe, the republic was proclaimed in Barcelona and then throughout Spain. But Franco's nationalist uprising soon plunged the country into civil war. In 1936, the International Brigades were formed, and fighters poured in from the whole continent to support the Spanish republic. In just a few years, revolutionary Catalonia became a hotbed of international proletarian struggle. Forced to leave Berlin and the central European countries after the beginning of the 1930s, many committed leftist psychoanalysts came to settle in Barcelona. François Tosquelles, a Catalonian psychiatrist and psychoanalyst, writes:

> It has been forgotten that Barcelona was a little Vienna between 1931 and 1936. I would like to pay tribute here to Professor Mira and to the group of psychiatrists and psychoanalysts from the most diverse schools who were brought to this city by the paranoid anxiety embodied by Nazism: Sándor Eiminder, Landsberg, Strauss, Brachfeld, and others.[1]

Tosquelles was actually trained by one of them, Sándor Eiminder, a Jewish Hungarian émigré, who was a pupil of Ferenczi and a companion of August Aichhorn in Vienna. Aichhorn and his psychoanalyst colleague, Siegfried Bernfeld, revolutionized the view of juvenile delinquency by considering the antisocial character of young people as a symptom to be treated by therapy rather than criminal punishment. It was through these men that the ideas of the Viennese psychoanalysts took root in Barcelona. The political, intellectual, and cultural competition that reigned in the city at the time was as fertile ground as 1920s Austria. In Spain, the anarchist syndicate had the majority; Pablo Casals performed "workers concerts"; many intellectuals supported the ongoing revolution, like Orwell, who described the Catalonian capital in this way:

> the aspect of Barcelona was something startling and overwhelming. It was the first time that I had ever been in a town where the working class was in the saddle. [...] Every shop and café had an inscription saying that it had been collectivized; even the bootblacks had been collectivized and their boxes painted red and black. [...] All this was queer and moving. [...] Above all, there was a belief in the revolution and the future, a feeling of having suddenly emerged into an era of equality and freedom. Human beings were trying to behave as human *beings* and not as cogs in the capitalist machine.[2]

In Catalonia, psychoanalysis found a new home conducive to its expansion and its necessary freedom to practice. Tosquelles would become a prominent representative, charting other paths than the "adaptation" promoted by Jones in Germany. Paradoxically, the context of the war was a major contributor to the technical innovations he developed and gave his trajectory specificity: A wartime clinician, Tosquelles had to organize the survival of the patients in his care. This is why he was not *primarily* concerned with the status of the treatment (which, incidentally, was impossible to carry out in wartime) but instead with therapeutic action to be taken on the social environment. From the outset, he was asking collective and political questions. For the clinician, it is not just a matter of providing therapy *in* the environment of the patients in his care but of actively participating in the complete overhaul of this environment—for example, the segregation to which these patients are subjected. From this point of view, it was the Catalonia commune's very political conditions, to which we shall return, that made his action possible and made it a therapeutic model. We shall see that Tosquelles's experience was foundational to the clinical work Oury and Guattari carried out with their patients at La Borde clinic in France. The eventual idea of "institutional psychotherapy" and its founding principle that "before claiming to treat the patient, we must treat the institution" were rooted in the Catalan experience.

The Context of the Spanish Revolution

In 1921, Primo de Rivera established his dictatorship in Spain and in Catalonia. The resistance gradually organized around the anarchists in the National Confederation of Labor (CNT, Confederación Nacional del Trabajo) and the Iberian Anarchist Federation (FAI), as well as the Catalan-Baleriac Communist Federation, which included the Worker and Peasant Bloc that Tosquelles had been a member of since he was 15. These different revolutionary currents were particularly alien to the centralizing line of the Spanish Communist Party, which was subservient to Moscow. Tosquelles recalls:

> I was a member of the Catalan-Baleriac Federation. At one point, Stalin sent us a guy, a Black man called Bréa. I will always remember those secret official envoys under Soviet control. This guy wanted us to go to Madrid, to make propaganda in Spain—where the monarchy and the military were in power—and to say: "All Power to the Soviets." No republicans, no anarchists, no socialists, nothing. "All Power to the Soviets." So two or three of us—not the Party, because it would not have done so officially—wrote to Stalin: my dear comrade, you are a very important Leader, but you don't understand what is happening here at all. In Spain, there are no soviets. Thus, saying "all-power-to-the-soviets" really proves the military and the king right. Bullshit. Worse. Besides, we won't speak Castilian because the Castilians are our oppressors. If you want similar propaganda to "all-power-to-the-soviets," you should say, "all-power-to-las-peñas." *Las peñas* are the bistros, the bistro discussions, those who wage war in the cafés. In the past, when you went to the café, whether in France or in Spain, you spent the whole day there, since the most important thing was to work as little as possible. So, as soon as you finished working, you had to go to the

café. You didn't go to get drunk or to form parties, but to discuss. There were guys on the right, the center, and the left, and we spoke for hours to remake the world.[3]

With his earthy humor, Tosquelles recalls here the extent of the divisions and the complexity of the geopolitical situation in which the Catalan revolutionaries were caught up. The Catalan leftist parties and Tosquelles's communist leanings defended an idea of open, libertarian communism, closer to the anarcho-communism and feminist communism to the left of Trotsky than to Russian Stalinism. Moreover, for the revolutionaries and for Tosquelles himself, this communism was only conceivable in the context of a much older struggle for Catalonian independence, and for "its Mediterranean, industrial, and democratic politics" against the yoke of Castille's "inquisitorial and authoritarian feudalism"[4]—Primo de Rivera being only the latest embodiment. Far from being just jokes, Tosquelles's advice to Stalin highlighted the blindness of out-of-touch communist propaganda, which Reich had also denounced in another context: It is quite simply impossible to make propaganda in Castilian because that is the language of the historic "oppressors"! And from the point of view of society's concrete practices and realities, the café is certainly the most conducive place for effective propaganda. It was not so much a matter of convincing the Castilians (how could that be?) as one of uniting the Catalan people in their diverse political components under the banner of the proletarian revolution. For no one then was unaware of the international dimension of the challenge, certainly not Tosquelles: "At the start of the war, no one could fail to recognize the specific scenario of class struggle, then grounded in the present. Moreover, class struggle as the most concrete aspect of the universal dynamic of history was present everywhere in 1936."[5]

Tosquelles's Therapeutic Action during the War

Driven by wartime necessities and concerned with the lives of his patients, Tosquelles had to innovate constantly. On the Aragon front in 1936, as part of the antifascist militias of the POUM, of which he was a founding member, he was appointed head of psychiatric services "in a vast area—specifically including Castille, the outskirts of Toledo, Extremadura and the north of Andalusia."[6] He was twenty-four. The material contingencies forced him to operate an outpatient clinic outside of the hospital, which was reminiscent of the clinical outpost Reich created in working-class neighborhoods. The aim was not to isolate the patient by locking them up, which would have the familiar consequence of making the illness chronic. Tosquelles recalls:

> What did I do in Aragon? I didn't have many patients; I prevented them from being sent 200 kilometers away from the front line; I treated them where things had been triggered, less than 15 kilometers away, according to a principle that could resemble that of the sector policy. If you send a war neurotic 150 kilometers from the front line, you will make it a chronic case. You can only treat them near the family where there has been trouble.[7]

Above all, Tosquelles had to "handle" the doctors, from both clinical and revolutionary perspectives:

> The civil war brought a change of perspective on the world. Doctors ordinarily have the stability of a bourgeois lifestyle in their heads. They are petit or grand bourgeois who want to live alone and make money, to be scientists. But in a civil war like ours, the doctor had to accept a change of perspective on the world; the doctor had to accept that it was the clients who determined the practice, and the doctor is not all-powerful. So I handled the psychotherapy of normal men to avoid crisis. You cannot perform psychiatry in a sector or in a hospital if you maintain a bourgeois, individualist ideology.[8]

As we can see, for Tosquelles the revolutionary ideal was embodied in a specific organization where the social division of medical work is challenged. At the same time, between 1936 and 1938, in the towns and countryside of Aragon and Catalonia, millions of POUM and anarchist peasants and workers profoundly transformed the relations of power and property. As shown by Langer's account, the women were not to be outdone, and they occupied a decisive position in these emancipatory movements. Economic production was entirely reorganized and money abolished in some communes.[9] During this period, Tosquelles created a therapeutic community in Almodovar del Campo. As director, he organized the recruitment of care staff, avoiding the inclusion of psychiatrists. Against specialization and the social division of labor, his clinic was intended for the people. The aim was to integrate care into the life of the city, and to organize this care with its members in all their heterogeneity:

> I chose lawyers who were afraid to go to war but who had never treated a madman, painters, literary men, whores. [...] Some of these whores turned into goddamned nurses. Extraordinary, isn't it? And because of their experience with men, they knew that everyone is crazy—even the men who go to whores—their professional training was quick. In a month, a whore, a lawyer, and a priest could become someone extraordinary. So all of my activities involved setting up sector and therapeutic communities, lobbying local politicians, the guys who represented some power in the country. That's what this sector activity was all about![10]

The Model of the Comarcas

From the POUM and the anarchists' perspective, a revolution was needed in the here and now: There was no question of waiting for the "great revolution" [le grand soir] or the centralizing figure of a party or a leader—quite the opposite. This was the principle of the local Catalan communes, or *comarcas*, the rural or urban communities where people reorganized daily social life. Their creation of course fell within an internationalist horizon: "This was the Spanish War, not a localized civil war, but one with a universal dimension, aiming at the seizure of power by the proletariat."[11] This horizon was a thousand miles away from the reactionary dogma Stalin imposed in this period. Some Russian fighters sent by Moscow to

Spain were not fooled and, recognizing real communism, betrayed their hierarchy to join the fighting in the Catalan-Spanish commune.

The Spanish Communist Party (PCE), obedient to Stalin, took a dim view of these libertarian experiments and undertook a veritable counter-revolution within the revolution. The party soon banned women from carrying and using weapons, reintroduced ranks and hierarchical ceremony in the army, and returned land and factories to their owners, as long as they were anti-Franco. The agricultural collectives were destroyed and, with the support of the republican army, the PCE proceeded to massacre anarchists and POUMists. Tosquelles attests:

> The Generalitat of Catalunya itself had lost all real power in the conduct of the war and in Catalonian political life, when the central government, more or less armed and inspired by the Spanish Communist Party, violently imposed itself, in the style of the well-known events under Stalin, on the powerful and originally anarchist workers' movement in Barcelona, and on the very firmly rooted Catalonian proletarian movement, as well as the Worker's Party for Marxist Unification (POUM)—often referred to at the time as Trotskyist.[12]

To top it off, Juan Negrín's Spanish government, which made re-establishing good relations with France and Britain a priority, dissolved the International Brigades. For Tosquelles, this decision rang the death knell for the proletarian revolution, in the interest of war among nations:

The International Brigades, present mainly on the Madrid front, withdrew from the fighting and were dissolved in December 1938, right in the middle of the battle of the Ebro, on the southern edge of Catalonia. Having thus removed the proletariat from the movement of history, everything was ready for the great war of the states—which began for France in September 1939. You know the rest.[13]

From Sept-Fons to Saint-Alban

In February 1939 the *Retirada*, the exodus of refugees from the war, began—then exile. On February 7, Hermann, a journalist at the *Populaire*, described it as follows: "No one who was at the Perthus today will be able to forget this extraordinary vision: a whole people, preferring exile to slavery, has been marching without cease, without haste, without cries, since the early morning hours."[14] For the historian Geneviève Dreyfus-Armand, "It was the largest exodus ever to take place at a French border."[15] In March, Madrid fell, which signed the death warrant for the Spanish Republic. Tosquelles moved to France thanks to the network set up by his wife. He was interned at Sept-Fons, one of the many concentration camps thrown together by the French government to isolate the 450,000 Spanish refugees. The conditions of detention were atrocious. The refugees were held in open air. It rained; it was freezing cold. No shelter, no latrines, the prisoners relieved themselves on the ground. Diseases soon struck and killed: typhoid, scabies, tuberculosis, or if not then hunger or the cold. The French administration, hostile to the arrival of these refugees, neglected and abused the detainees: It encouraged them to return to Spain, improving the lot in the camps of those who accepted. In order to avoid demonstrations of solidarity by the French soldiers with the Spanish refugees, contingents from colonial armies were posted to oversee the camps. Support movements organized regardless, and some refugees managed to escape.

In the Sept-Fons camp, Tosquelles created a psychiatric service:

> In this service, too, it was very funny. Once again, there were political militants, painters, guitarists ... There was only one psychiatric nurse; all the others were normal people. The service I created was very effective. I think it's one of the places where I did some really good psychiatry, in that concentration camp, in the mud. It was magnificent. And on the other hand, it was used to provoke escapes ... and other such exploits. It is often overlooked that the Spanish republicans who escaped the camps provided the backbone of the Resistance throughout southwest France.[16]

Tosquelles knew what he was talking about: On January 6, 1940, he joined the psychiatric hospital Saint-Alban in Lozère, which he turned into a major site of resistance. Recruited as assistant nurse, he immediately set about to transform the facility, which was dilapidated and in a bad state. Saint-Alban was itself a small poor and isolated village. The sick, watched over by poorly trained nuns, were confined inside the hospital, even though it was located in the heart of the city. But the war disrupted this ordinary segregation and made it possible for Tosquelles to subvert it. Conditions being more precarious than ever, necessity made law: Opening up the hospital to the city allowed for trading services with the farmers in the surrounding areas. Elsewhere, mentally ill people were condemned to die of severe nutritional deficiencies: During the Occupation and the Vichy regime, more than half of hospitalized patients died of hunger. It was a massacre.[17] But the patients at Saint-Alban escaped this doomed fate thanks to the struggle for survival waged there. Tosquelles highlights the political effects:

> The patients, the nurses, and even bursars and doctors, waged the struggle against hunger, got out of the hospital, went to the peasants to get butter and turnips in exchange for some work. We connected patients to the outside world, not to wage war, but to trade on the black market. We organized mushroom exhibitions to teach them how to forage. And since there were food cards for tuberculosis patients, we invented a tuberculosis ward. When a guy started having hunger edemas, suddenly a diagnosis of tuberculosis was made. There was a whole chain of things, which meant that, ultimately, war only came at the right time ... and the Resistance too.[18]

Many refugees, including some who were illegal migrants, reached Saint-Alban: Tristan Tzara, Paul Éluard, Georges Canguilhem, Henri Matarasso, and Victor Bardach found refuge there. Since June 1942, Éluard had directed the publisher Éditions de Minuit: Saint-Alban served then as a launching pad for a significant number of the books printed in Saint-Flour. Lucien Bonnafé, a communist, was appointed head physician in 1943. Frantz Fanon also came to train there after the war.[19] Thus during the worst years of Pétain and the Nazi occupation, psychoanalysis, Marxism, and poetry crossed paths in this place. An intense communitarian life was organized around the meetings of a secret society, the Gévaudan Society. As told by Danièle Sicadon, Jean-Claude Polack and François Pain, psychoanalysts who worked at La Borde: "at night, waiting for a visitor or a weapons airdrop, organizing care for the wounded or putting together secret publications, these meetings started building the world of the asylum, which was already busy 'healing life.' This was during the Gévaudan Society, named after the famous and elusive beast [a man-eating animal rumored to be behind attacks in the region the eighteenth century]."[20] The patients knew that Resistance fighters were hidden on the third floor of the château. The mother superior was also an accomplice of Tosquelles, and there were even reports that "the weapons of the Gévaudan underground were hidden under her enormous bed!"[21]

At Saint-Alban, the revolutionary organization obviously affected all social relations, and above all, the relations with patients. Opening the hospital to the outside world required a radical transformation of the facility's internal operating processes to make it into an "institution."[22] This meant changing the habit of segregation and fighting against violence and disdain towards the patients. To this end, Tosquelles set up the "club," "a self-managed system, if you want to use that language. We engaged in self-management and its practices here." The club, which formally served as the editorial board for the newspaper *Trait-d'union*, was actually the "most important collective psychotherapy site in the hospital." A transversal arrangement bringing together caregivers and patients, it took charge of the daily collective organization of the institution, constituting a powerful instrument for subverting the rules promoted by the bourgeois contractualist state. It was also an effective, concrete provider for both psychological and institutional care; it was not to be confined to a particular activity but instead extended to the entire hospital, its sites, and its functions. In this, Saint-Alban was inspired by the famous *comarcas* established during the Catalan revolution. This revolutionary experiment would be revived by Jean Oury and Félix Guattari, who tried to draw out all of its consequences when they founded La Borde clinic in 1953. "There was no point in being at La Borde if you didn't know about the POUM,"[23] Oury regularly said, suggesting a continuity with the experience of the Spanish commune. Until the end of his life, Oury claimed to be a POUMist.[24] Especially at La Borde, the consequences of this radical approach were soon to be further developed and problematized in a new way for psychoanalysis.

The Post-War Context in France and the Founding of La Borde

The clinic in postwar France cannot be considered outside of the political issues that, from 1945 to the 1970s, continued to drive a large part of the French psychiatric-analytic community. While in many countries psychoanalysis had to adapt at the price of repressing its political dimension—whether we think of Marie Langer's setbacks in South America or psychoanalysis's fate in the United States after the exile of the Viennese analysts[25]—in France the experiment of a politically committed psychoanalysis inherited from Red Vienna continued. Indeed, for the politicized psychiatrists and psychoanalysts, often Marxists who took part in the Resistance, the war was not truly over in Saint-Alban and elsewhere. Of course, Nazism and fascism had been defeated, but their own struggle certainly did not aim for the restoration of bourgeois society. They had fought and resisted in the name of achieving a communist society.[26] Those who had fought in Spain and had been through Saint-Alban also had concrete experience of revolutionary transformation and its decisive effects on patient care. For these therapists, the struggle must continue against the bourgeoisie and its repressive organization of psychiatry, one of its key components being the segregation of the mad within institutions, where paradoxically, some of them were responsible as medical directors.

In the immediate postwar period, many working groups independent of state institutions were formed. A first was set up in 1945, and included, among others Julian de Ajuriaguerra, Lucien Bonnafé, Georges Daumézon, Louis Le Guillant, Henri Ey, Jacques Lacan, and François Tosquelles. Just like the collective of mathematicians that published its work under the name Bourbaki, this group was named "Doctor Batia," which means "hope" in Basque. It split up in 1947, the year that the young Jean Oury arrived at Saint-Alban for his training. At this time, the hospital had a prestigious aura. Its ties with the Resistance were well known, which attracted the new generation of interns to which Oury belonged. Oury brought with him the latest concepts of Jacques Lacan, whom he had heard develop the thesis of "psychic causality" at the Bonneval Congress the previous year: "I was seeing all these people parade around talking, and then in May I heard this guy, and I said to myself, finally someone smart; it was Lacan, and it was a relief."[27] In 1953, he began analytic treatment with Lacan, which lasted until Lacan's death in 1980.

Figure 5 François Tosquelles, Jean Oury and Gisela Pankow in Milan in 1975

Born in 1924 into a modest background, Jean Oury was steeped in the experience of the *banlieue rouge* [communist neighborhoods in France] of his birth, La Garenne-Colombes.[28] He participated in youth movements that were very active in the Liberation, and he forged a libertarian sensibility. When he arrived at Saint-Alban, he had an immediate affinity with Tosquelles. In his words, this encounter formed the "crucible," the "matrix" for the later founding of the La Borde clinic.[29] In 1950, Oury took over responsibility for the Saumery clinic in Loir-et-Cher. He brought in people from his own background, militants from his neighborhood and friends, to help him organize daily life with the patients. Félix Guattari, six years his junior, joined him for short periods, on the recommendation of Jean's brother, the educator Fernand Oury. At this time, Guattari was studying pharmacology, which bored him. He was fascinated by Jean Oury, who became his "moral confessor." Oury invited him to read Lacan, whose writings enthralled him, and encouraged him to resume the studies in philosophy he had initially intended.[30] Guattari, who had been active in the Communist Party since he was fifteen and frequented the youth hostels, had a similar social and political background to Oury. For Guattari, Saumery was the starting point for uninterrupted discussions with the clinic's director.

Strongly influenced by Tosquelles's teaching, Oury set about transforming the patients' environment at Saumery to break them out of the ordinary social segregation to which they were subjected. In 1953, when the owners indicated their desire to take back control of the clinic, Oury decided to move with all of his patients a few kilometers away in the isolated and dilapidated château that he had bought, which became the La Borde clinic. From its creation, the question of power was tackled head-on. The founding text from 1953—called ironically, "Constitution of Year I"—argued for a "complete overhaul: of the existing structures in a traditional organization; of the ideas that each member might have of their functions." Three general principles were defined: democratic centralism, changing of positions, and community organizing of work, all of which ran counter to the classic psychiatric system.

> In this way, it [the text, "Constitution of Year 1"] is a complete break with all the traditions of the hospital (hierarchical and non-democratic), of the syndicate (protected and coded professional status), and of commerce (the community begins here by pooling salaries). It is impossible not to notice—in fact the text largely authorizes it—the political resonance of these three axes: Leninist for decisions and execution, Trotskyist and libertarian for the struggle against bureaucratization, and for communization.[31]

Given the vitality of the political-clinical debates in the psychoanalytic community at this time, Oury's founding of the La Borde clinic was quickly recognized by his peers. As early as 1954, Louis Le Guillant, Évelyne Kenstemberg, and Georges Daumézon came there to meet Oury and sent patients his way.[32]

Oury played an increasingly important role in debates within his discipline. His politically engaged practice and thinking came to foster a new group of psychiatrists-psychoanalysts, created in 1957 in the lineage of Doctor Batia's group. The Sèvres group, formed on Daumézon's initiative was more extensive than its predecessor; it integrated the new generation of psychiatrists-psychoanalysts who had reached positions of responsibility in the meantime (such as Oury, Guattari, Paul-Claude Racamier, etc.). Its founding document made no secret of its political orientation, wholeheartedly assuming the revolutionary ambition of the immediate postwar years: "There is no revolution without revolutionary doctrine, there is no revolution without party, both stemming from a lucid analysis of the situation we are living in."[33]

But a disagreement soon broke out among the members of the Sèvres group. Let's pause for a moment to consider this revealing argument. Indeed, it opens the way for a new revolutionary heuristic approach to the recognition, analysis, and use of unconscious phenomena that necessarily accompany any institution, and poses the question of the role psychoanalysis can and must play in it.

Political and Clinical Stakes

First of all, let's remember that La Borde clinic's revolutionary organization was not just political. Indeed, it was not dissociated from the patient's therapeutic needs, and it also supported the principle of extending psychoanalysis to the whole institution. During the war, Tosquelles had already involved sex workers and priests in his undertaking: He had shown that the care provided to patients was better when the social division of labor and its specialization were suspended. To put it another way, the radical transformation of power relations in the hospital was all the more imperative since, structurally, they had a direct negative effect on mental illness. It was therefore necessary to conduct a critique of the classical psychiatric hospital and its key figure, the psychiatrist. As Guattari said later, psychiatric hospitals are "radically diverted from their apparent social aim," which is to provide treatment. In fact,

> these enormous concentration camp machines [machineries concentrationnaires] increase the opacity of disturbances, the solitude of the patients, the nonsense of their existence. The reaction they provoke is a social pathoplasty of mental illness, causing them to harden and close in on themselves. This social alienation is superposed on the more specific instances of a psychopathological alienation.[34]

The social conditions in which the patient lives—particularly in the so-called care environment, the psychiatric hospital—reinforce their mental illness.

In a way, we are back at one of the classic problems facing the politically engaged analyst: At the intersection between their analytic practice and the often socially overdetermined distress they encounter and that they must treat with inappropriate, even harmful means. It was therefore necessary to unmask the psychiatric institution's hypocritical pretense, and, for the therapist, to analyze the hospital's contradictory functions. This was a basic requirement for any claim to "treat," and the whole point of the concept Oury coined, *double alienation*, social and mental. At La Borde clinic, therapy was not only individual but also institutional. Psychoanalysis had to be deployed on these two levels. Oury and Guattari would thus transform analytic technique and extend its scope to the social environment in order to improve the patient's psychic condition. It was necessary to "determine that conditions that allow an institution to play an analytic role in the Freudian sense."[35]

This approach disrupted the inherited postwar psychiatry. It was far from unanimous among members of the movement, which were beginning to come together under the term "institutional psychotherapy" proposed by Daumézon in 1952. The drive to reform asylum psychiatry in the interest of sector psychiatry would only be achieved years later, mainly because of major differences of opinion on psychoanalysis and its scope.[36] Without going into the intricacies of internal debates on this question, let us just summarize some of the changes brought about by the practice at La Borde, which were at the root of the controversy that would cause the Sèvres group to implode in 1959. It was not only that psychiatrists, as representatives of the power delegated by the bourgeois state, had to carry out their own critique, but also the preferred therapeutic tools at their disposal, like psychoanalysis, had to be shared—including with their colleagues who were not legally or symbolically authorized to appropriate this knowledge, like nurses. Finally, psychoanalysis itself had to break out of the bourgeois framework of the cure in order to extend to the institution as a whole. From there, it had to be in a position to unmask group fantasies, such as the identification with the leader described by Freud, fantasies that contribute greatly to making the institution sick and, as a consequence, aggravate the patients' suffering.

Within the Sèvres group, René Diatkine and Paul-Claude Racamier[37] did not share this vision at all. On the contrary, they wished to reserve for doctors alone the right to practice psychoanalysis in a hospital; for them there was no question of nurses having access to it. Nor did they intend to generalize psychoanalysis to the institution. This disagreement caused the group to implode in 1959— even though at La Borde they had been experimenting for several years already with the generalization of psychoanalysis to the whole institution and its members, and the beneficial effects—both clinical and political—could be observed *in situ*. In the wake of Tosquelles's critique of psychiatric power and its alienating and iatrogenic effects, Oury and Guattari privileged the analytic model and its transversality. For them, psychoanalysis must not reinforce the psychiatrist's power; quite the opposite, it must call into question psychiatry and the psychiatrist's place. Albeit in an entirely different context, this debate, with Diatkine and Racamier on one side, and Oury and Guattari on the other, recalls the dispute that had divided analysts in the mid-1920s about extending psychoanalysis to the whole of society and the political implications of psychoanalysis.

Analysis in Psychiatry

"The understanding of unconscious content, drives, conflicts, is likely to be infinitely more trying than useful," and could lead to "an eroticization of the staff," an "even worse depressive reaction," "a devaluation of words and affects leading to a rejection as dangerous as the rejection in the nosology": these were Diatkine's unequivocal warnings during the final meeting of the Sèvres groups, regarding the "dangerous" relations of the nurse to psychoanalysis. The nurse's closeness with the patient, far from being a resource, constituted an additional contraindication: "by the very nature of their position and function, the nursing staff is particularly pushed and their mental integrity is always attacked."[38] They must therefore be protected from unconscious knowledge so as not to be "pushed" even further. According to him, psychoanalysis is not recommended for the nurse's work, and is instead the psychiatrist's principal tool, their "new science." The psychiatrist has the monopoly on it and is its representative in the institution, its only carrier. The psychoanalytic doctor's identification with power is therefore valued and assumed: "first and foremost, the psychoanalyst brings a model of identification to young psychiatrists as well as the surrounding caregivers in the institution."[39] And following Freud's analysis of the army and the church,[40] the system's operability is founded on the supremacy of the identification with the leader, embodied by the psychiatrist-psychoanalyst.[41] The introduction of psychoanalysis to the hospital aims first of all to pull psychiatry out of its crisis. As a "true science," it is "more effective" for breaking psychiatry out of its impasse, starting by restoring medical authority: "You won't get anywhere until you have restored medical authority; only then can you share it."[42]

The eventual sharing of authority in the future hangs on the personality of the psychiatrist-psychoanalyst, of whom Racamier gives a brief portrait: "Stripped of Olympian attributes, the psychoanalyst offers an example of tolerance without masochism, of presence without complacency, of firmness without false poise, acceptance and controlled use of personal affective reactions, and finally of curiosity without impatience."[43] The psychoanalytic doctor's psychology is elevated here to the status of the institution's regulating ideal. Psychoanalysis becomes the new medical norm and the psychiatrist-psychoanalyst its medium. But as Robert Castel writes:

> By reducing the issue of psychiatry to a crisis of knowledge and authority, this attempt ultimately falls short of the analysis proposed by the initiators of the first attempts to reform psychiatry, who at least had the merit of seeing that transforming the institutional structure required something quite different than replacing one medical theory with another medical theory, even if it were psychoanalytically inspired.[44]

We can better understand the tautological operation allowing the nurse to be excluded and through which psychoanalysis, led astray, provides an ideological justification for the psychiatric order. Its "reign" over the institution is not only perfectly consistent with the division of labor within psychiatry but also makes psychiatry operative. "Psychiatry's all-purpose maid," psychoanalysis becomes its new ideological mask. But then, Castel continues, "we spare ourselves from analyzing [these roles] in their specificity and their contradictory purposes; it is above all a convenient way to avoid asking the fundamental sociological question: in the name of what (or whom) does psychiatry-psychoanalysis serve as a model, whose authority does it delegate?"[45]

As you can imagine, Diatkine and his approach was bound to clash with La Borde's conception, derived from POUMist heritage and elaborated against bourgeois psychoanalysis and psychiatry. Thus, the question of the doctor's status and relationship to the nurse crystallizes many issues. In a 1955 text, Oury and Guattari, in the form of a discussion, unmask the inherent power relations in the psychiatric enterprise and offer a critique of medical power. For Oury,

> We should begin by defining the relationships that exist between doctors and nurses, with all of their mystical implications... . Félix: Doctors ... bolster and are responsible for the mystification, and as such, they reflect their class ideology ... I think that the problem must not be too distinct from class relationships, but completely fundamental.[46]

They target the psychiatrist in particular: Their relation to the nurse is fundamentally a class relation. The figure of the psychiatrist and the power delegated to psychiatry fit well with an ideological enterprise aiming to maintain relations of domination:

> Oury: It is obvious that the role of the doctor is to be a defender of state institutions. He or she [*sic*] is empowered by the state to ensure that hospital rules are followed without intervening in its economic-social structure. The role necessarily implies that he or she be respected so that patients are presented with the perfect image of respect and dignity. There is some typical

clowning around, since it is a reflection of the society in which nurses work.[47]

"Officially" called upon to "treat" people, the hospital is first the site of an exclusionary power, and the psychiatrist is an essential part, as guarantor of the rules of the institution. Contrary to what Racamier advocated, it is necessary to reveal the subterfuge that makes up medical authority rather than reproducing it, and worse still, giving it a foundation in the practice of psychoanalysis. For this authority only really exists to conceal the relations of domination in which both the nurse and the patient remain prisoners. This is how we should understand La Borde's call "to get rid of doctors as the individuals, colleagues, citizens who offer to 'speak for ... ,' to be the 'spokesperson' of the subject that the institution could be."[48] Representing the state and its order, the microcosm of the asylum concentrates and exacerbates social contradictions, which is why a deep analysis is needed:

> Oury: In this supervision of madmen, you could say that there is the "view from the outside," the "view from the inside" and the "madmen's view." The traditional view from the outside, for example, is the idea that the more education you receive, the longer you go to school, the more you can understand madmen: you have to be a doctor. While those at the bottom of the nurses' ladder, uneducated in principle, cannot understand anything. There is a rationalism in society that is more of a rationalization of bad faith, of nastiness. The view from the inside is the relationship with madmen

> on a daily basis, on the condition of breaking a certain "contract" with tradition. You could say, in a sense, that knowing what being in contact with madmen is like is also being progressive.
>
> Félix: We could even say that awareness of this "contract with tradition" and the decision to break with it are the conditions for a phenomenological approach to madness.[49]

Breaking from within the "traditional contract" that places the nurse in a subordinate relationship with the doctor because they don't have access to psychoanalytic knowledge (they are "uneducated") challenges the psychiatric contract and its law, which excludes the mad; but above all it also makes it possible to encounter the mad person in new coordinates.[50] Here, the critique of the division of labor joins with analytic therapy of psychosis. The aim is precisely the possibility of true contact between nurses and patients: "Nurses ... often consider themselves to be third-rate doctors, despite their privileged and often irreplaceable therapeutic power."[51] This implies a revolution both of the institution *and* of subjectivity. The break with the bourgeois contract form, which reifies both the figure of the psychiatrist and of the nurse in the division of psychiatric labor, becomes the condition for access to madness and treating it with institutional therapy. All of the roles are redefined, beginning with the doctor's:

> Institutional therapy radically modifies the medical profession's work habits. The doctor at La Borde is not just asked to write prescriptions, administer electroshocks,

or monitor the progress of insulin treatment: they are also asked to take an interest in the way the club is organized, the work in the workshops, in what is going on in the institutional field. The doctor is not only asked to be a representative of medical knowledge, they are also asked to be an occupational therapist. The same applies to all the staff at La Borde: the housekeeper, the nurse, the cook must be versatile; the gardener should know how to grow flowers, but must also be a caregiver.[52]

Analytic practice, freed from psychiatry's grip, becomes decidedly "progressive"; it even anticipates the implementation of the coming revolution on the level of society. For Oury, the space of the asylum in a way crystallizes all social struggles:

> some people have been delegated by society to live with the mad, making them into a kind of rampart of people, a wall of heads, arms and legs to protect society from the mad. Let them manage as best they can as long as society remains peaceful. And all of society's struggles are inevitably reproduced in this wall, which is part of society.[53]

This is precisely why segregated psychiatry is the privileged place for revolutionary change, from which what Deleuze and Guattari later call a "materialist psychiatry" could be realized.[54]

The Revolution Achieved by Psychoanalysis

It is important to realize that the introduction of a rotation of tasks and functions, like the sharing of the therapeutic function, do not only aim to abolish the social division of labor. They also have crucial subjective and unconscious effects for the institution's members. As opposed to Racamier's recommendations, we have seen that the aim at La Borde was to deconstruct the figure of the psychiatrist. But what are the instructions for this? Guattari gives the broad outlines: The doctor must renounce imaginary identification with their role and its "basis of a phantasy alienation" in order "to effect the splitting-up of the medical function," transferring their real, legal power "into a number of different responsibilities involving various kinds of groups and individuals" "without retreating in panic."[55] For this, the first step is to "shift and disrupt the totalizing character of [the] institution"[56] by creating "vacuoles", that is, protected spaces where the institution's members can associate freely and question their role: "What the hell are we doing here?" These spaces represent a preliminary step for any attempt at group analysis: "a fundamental distinction will emerge from the very beginning between curing the alienation of the group and analyzing it."[57] Set up over the long term, a group system of this kind—where challenging and redefining roles are enshrined—is bound to have an effect on its subjects, beginning with the patient who can find an interpreting function here.[58] Through the concrete transformation of unequal psychiatric systems, the "reshaping of [the institution members'] ego ideals"[59] can be performed indirectly. A modification of the subject occurs in their relation with others as well as themselves, in particular their relation with the superego invested in the institution.

In 1957, when the Sèvres group was formed, the radical questioning of the nurse's status had thus already taken place in the practice at La Borde: The distinction between care staff and service staff was officially abolished. All the workers, with or without degrees, became "psychiatric monitors" and their salaries were equalized.[60] But declaring equality is not enough to achieve it, and the question is still being asked in the same terms today: How can a group in the institution of the asylum, whose strict hierarchy and social division of labor are often comparable to those in prison, gradually overcome the social injunctions and their alienations to the point where its members themselves assume and desire such a change? This is where psychoanalysis, extended to the whole institution, intervenes. It has no vanguardist pretentions of enlightening the masses and guiding them, but rather of creating in each group the right conditions for a social disalienation, so that, in return, "an analysis of desire, on oneself and on others" becomes possible.[61]

Let's pause for a moment to consider the paradigmatic case of Georgette, which, according to the authors of the La Borde monograph, forms a kind of "foundational myth."[62] From humble origins, Georgette, at first a service worker, ultimately became a monitor. Yet before that she was already providing care on a daily basis, to the point that she could have been mistaken for a nurse. The monograph authors ask: "Was Georgette caught in a new group field? Or was Georgette herself establishing a new field in the division of labor? Was Georgette a symbol of a mutation, a summary of what is transforming? Or was Georgette a false problem?"[63] In reality, as early as 1953, the more or less unofficial and spontaneous "interpenetration of services" was very much present, and it was not just Georgette: "Ariane comes down from the linen room to the workshops; Mademoiselle Paupinel, the model of a good nurse, sews; Lelond, who mainly runs drawing workshops, also works in the infirmary, Seito goes from the chicken coop to the pharmacy ...."[64] The official abolition of the difference between the noble care professions and those considered subordinate thus confirms an extensively tested previous mode of operation; it was not the result of a decision imposed by a revolutionary leadership. In this case, this decision was in part already subjectivized by the institution's members: It was effective because many of them wanted it. The same applies to former patients who subsequently became salaried psychiatric monitors—because they got better and proved to be competent. A rotation of tasks was thus officially put into place.

In keeping with this institutional dynamic, new analytic groups were created at La Borde. Caregiver/care-receiver discussion groups explicitly set themselves the aim of analyzing the institutional imaginary, which presupposed a number of extensions to classical psychoanalysis. It was not so much that it was "off the couch," to borrow Racamier's expression, but rather that it confronted the issue of group fantasy and its relation to the subject. Guattari's contribution here is decisive.

The Question of Group Phantasy in Guattari

As noted by both Freud and Lacan, groups set up rituals and draw their operability from the members' relationship to the leader, who occupies the place of the ego ideal. But for Guattari, groups are not only phantasmatic because they protect their subjects from a constitutive anxiety, related to a situation of infantile helplessness, through a substitute for the image of the father. The Other and the figures necessary for the subject are not just mythical: This phantasmization also reveals a political function. While it protects the subject from anxiety, it likewise consists in casting its social condition into the shadows, which it helps to fabricate. For example, in a profoundly alienated group like the hospital, the symbolically overdetermined "distorting imagery" that embraces both neurotic and psychotic patients enables "the neurotic [to] have his narcissism reinforced beyond his wildest hopes, while the psychotic can continue silently devoting himself to his sublime universal passions."[65] The group phantasy's misrecognition [méconnaissance] "protects" its subject from an "awareness" of its own condition but also reinforces its narcissistic identification with what society expects of it. In other terms, the operation of subjugation [assujettissement] is only possible because the subject themselves participates in this misrecognition of the group phantasy's symbolic nature. And the subject does so all the more willingly because, in return, the phantasy determines each person's places in the group, places where the subject "wants" to fit in. Thus the subject can think of themselves as the leader, doctor, or patient:

> Experience of institutional therapeutics makes it clear that individual phantasizing never respects the particular nature of this symbolic plane of group phantasy. On the contrary, it tries to absorb it, and to overlay it with

> particular imaginings that are "naturally" to be found in the various roles that could be structured by using the signifiers circulated by the collective. This "imaginary incarnation" of some of the signifying articulations of the group—on the pretext of organization, efficiency, prestige, or, equally, of incapacity, nonqualification, etc.—crystallizes the structure as a whole, hinders its possibilities for change, determines its features and its "mass," and restricts to the utmost its possibilities for dialogue with anything that might tend to bring its "rules of the game" into question: in short, it produces all the conditions for degenerating into what we have called a dependent group [groupe assujetti].[66]

In this process of the Imaginary of the subject, who unconsciously projects the coordinates of their own ego onto the group in order to appropriate it and situate themselves within the group according to the contingencies of its history and social determinations, makes the phantasmization process one of the psychic operators of alienation. Even if Freud "in all innocence" missed the situation's social reality through a "shift in plane" (since he ignored the political dimension of the phantasy's repressive function by relating it first and foremost to a problem of individual psychology), he did, however, lead us, as Guattari tells us, "to paths that may be more reliable than any others."[67] And that is why according to him, "no true revolutionary change can be achieved without psychoanalysis."[68] Indeed, the subjugated [assujetti] group's determination does not just affect its subjects abstractly and externally—in their function, their status—but tends towards a "totalization" that needs to be "toppled."[69]

Figure 6 Félix Guattari (copyright Bruno, Emmanuel, Stephen Guattari. Félix Guattari Archies/IMEC

The conscious and unconscious images, symbols, and representations that the subjects make of themselves, of others, and of the group are not independent from their concrete, phantasmatically overdetermined social conditions. This symbolic phantasmization of the group unique to a given situation needs to be analyzed: "a particular phantasy, originating within an individual or a particular group, becomes a kind of collective currency, put into circulation and providing a basis for group phantasizing [fantasmatisation]."[70]

This analysis is all the more necessary for Guattari because the subjugated groups do not only concern extreme situations, like dictatorships or sects, but also contemporary society and its institutions, like the hospital—where certain services form veritable miniature dictatorships. And, unless one subscribes to Freud's late anthropological pessimism and a suspicious view of groups and crowds, which are by "nature" subjugated, the analyst cannot stay in the office, wrapped up in the "bourgeois contractual" model of the classic cure. As a militant revolutionary, Guattari has a quite different knowledge of groups and crowds, and on many occasions he experienced cases where the crowd was not the blind mass described by Gustave Le Bon or in some of Freud's texts. So what happens in these moments of collective solidarity and mutual attention at the level of unconscious phenomena and the circulation of affects? Rather than dissolving the subject, can the group not instead precipitate it, reveal it? Don't we find "subject effects" in some of these groups? Guattari deepens psychoanalytic investigation on the basis of his own direct political experience of emancipation.

Far from limiting his descriptive analysis to the phenomena of leader identification—an approach that too often allows analysts to dismiss politics out of hand, and by extension, to reduce any group to the subjugation of its subjects—Guattari reflects on the emancipated group's subjectivity. Beyond Freud and Lacan, Guattari thus focuses his analysis on the possibility of non-subjugated groups. In the context of treatment [cure], Lacan, who was Guattari's analyst at the time, distinguished empty speech—a speechless discourse where the subject is absent—from full speech, where the subject can assume their desire and truth in order to transform themselves.[71] Guattari takes up the problem of truth and desire as they are defined in typical treatment [cure] and transposes them to the group framework. He then asks the following question: Under what conditions can full speech by the subject, as Lacan understands it, occur within a group? Guattari, who was able to observe such speech in his numerous group experiences, then puts forth the hypothesis that there are also subject groups, that is, those that allow the subject to reveal itself. From this, the question becomes how to bring about or encourage the emergence of such emancipatory groups. This is the whole idea of what Guattari calls transversality in psychoanalysis, which can be defined as the implementation of renewed analytic practice in the institution: a practice aiming to transform subjects and their relationship to the social structures they support by fostering the institutional conditions that can precipitate the advent of subject groups.

The Object of Psychoanalysis: From the objet petit "a" ...

It is from this political group conception of desire that Guattari, in the wake of Reich, tackles a preconceived idea inherited from the Marxist tradition, according to which power "lies" to the proletarian's consciousness to achieve its ends of domination. No, the masses have not been fooled, they desired fascism and its Führer. History is replete with examples in which the subject's desire has worked against it. Just think of the kamikaze, whose desire consists of a total social subjugation culminating in death.

Or even of the audience unanimously acquiescing, with enthusiastic fury, to Goebbel's proposal to declare "total war" in 1943.[72] Obviously, for the analyst this lethal desire that structures subjugated groups is only desire's mask. In these social formations saturated with images of obedience, all "speech" "tips over into slogans." The conscious and unconscious images, symbols, and representations that subjects make of themselves, others, and the group tend to reify its members. Under the overwhelming effect of the superego, the subjects of the subjugated group, like their individual fantasies, are very inconsistent. They are one with the group [font corps avec]:

> they are not fundamentally part of anything outside the group and it is a sheer accident that they have fallen back on that particular "body" [corps propre]—an alienating and laughable fiction, the justification of an individual driven into solitude and anxiety precisely because society misunderstands and represses the real body and its desire.[73]

The subject's psychic fragility in its relation to the subjugated group is such that its very body is threatened with being but a "laughable fiction." The group represses the real body and singular desire. What does this mean?

We have seen that the subject is all the more fragile since the group superego demands its members' submission in order to constitute its empire by totalizing the force of each member. It does not derive its power from the mere force of its insignia. And if this dispossession/alienation touches the most intimate part of the subject, it is because it not only concerns its image but also its *jouissance*. The group is plugged into the very bodies of its subjects that it subjects to its imaginary law; but in return, and as if by compensation, the subject obtains a powerful *jouissance* from belonging to this group order. As Guattari and Deleuze write later:

> A form of social production and reproduction, along with its economic and financial mechanisms, its political formations, and so on, can be desired as such, in whole or in part, independently of the interests of the desiring-subject. It was not by means of a metaphor, even a paternal metaphor, that Hitler was able to sexually arouse the fascists. It is not by means of a metaphor that a banking or stock-market transaction, a claim, a coupon, a credit, is able to arouse people who are not necessarily bankers. And what about the effects of money that grows, money that produces more money? There are socioeconomic "complexes" that are also veritable complexes of the unconscious, and that communicate a voluptuous wave from the top to the bottom of their hierarchy (the military-industrial complex).[74]

This question of the subject's *jouissance* had already been elaborated by Lacan in the 1950s in his seminar on the register of the real, which Guattari attended, an investigation he would deepen until the end of his teaching. For Lacan, even philosophy's clear, distinct thinking is supported by an enjoyment (*un jouir*), hence his transliteration of Descartes' "*je suis*/I am" into "*je souis*" [a combination of *suis* and *jouis*].[75] Beyond images and words, beyond the imaginary and the symbolic, another register is articulated to structure the subject: that of the real and its *jouissance*. Lacan first locates this register in the *infans*'s first indistinct relationships to the maternal Other—what Freud names in *An Outline* the "Thing" (*das Ding*)—or the maternal body escaping any possible judgment by the toddler who cannot speak. The domain of the Thing (which Lacan once called "*a*chose" in a single word [condensing objet petit *a* and the Thing) is also the domain of the first non-representable *jouissances* of an immature child [un petit d'homme] undifferentiated from its environment. Lacan extracts from this what he calls the object *a*. Without merging with the Thing, whose trace it bears, the object *a* takes its place, as its substitute. The object *a* is non-representable, only grasped in the form of "partial objects" of the body: the object of sucking—the breast, the object of excreting—the feces, the voice, the gaze.[76] It is the cause of the subject's desire insofar as it is the vector of its fantasies and representations. Placing the subject in a position of "internal exclusion from its object," the object *a* exceeds the logic of the symbolic and the imaginary, while enabling their articulation.

For Guattari, the relevance of Lacan's analysis of the function of the object *a* is precisely that it can account for the subject's desire in groups. In fact, he distinguishes a dialectic of the subject's imaginary relations to the group in terms of partial objects: This dialectic conditions the subjugated group's operativity and the phantasy's effectiveness. The subject is suspended in the group phantasy because there is transference of the subject's partial objects onto the group:

this embodying of the individual phantasy upon the group, or this latching on of the individual to the group phantasy, transfers onto the group the damaging effect of those partial objects—*objet petit a*—described by Lacan as the oral or anal object, the voice, the look and so on, governed by the totality of the phallic function.[77]

The group finds its real operability in its subjects' partial objects that it shapes. The group phantasy draws its strength from these non-representable body fragments and their archaic virulence. Swarming behind the attraction of its phallic and agalmatic image (the substitute image of the father, for example) are the partial objects it turns to its own advantage. The repression that the group exercises on its subjects stems from its takeover of the apparatus of the drives. The subject's alienation by the group is thus "totalizing": it is no less imaginary than real, and also symbolic, albeit in different proportions. Moreover, the subjugated group's symbols are poor and cartoonish—think of those of the Nazis—and this symbolic poverty explains the subject's imaginary fragility all the more because the demands of its real drive-based body are exacerbated.

Guattari observes that the neurotic, and even paranoid, processes that accompany the "extraordinary way that bureaucratization took place in the Bolshevik Party [...] become more violent as the instincts underlying them are more powerful."[78] Subjugated groups are thus fundamentally unstable, because of the splitting they create in their subjects: "identification with the prevailing images of the group is by no means always static, for the badge of membership often has links with narcissistic and death instincts that it is hard to define."[79] Through the imposition of its univocal law, the subjugated group's "ideal" exacerbates the subject's intrapsychic tensions. This means that, constitutively, the group's power is also its weakness. The real of the body and the drives disrupts the group's totalitarian and imaginary law. Yet it is precisely because of these cleavages, which it is possible to analyze, that the subjugated group may be "in a position to escape from its corporized and spatializing phantasy representation."[80]

... to the "objet b"

But can we push the analyses further and, in the manner of the object *a* as a vector of phantasy, make the assumption that there is a real group object behind the group phantasy? Oury raises this question of "the real group object" and defers to Lacan: "I spoke with Lacan about it at the time; perhaps not the object 'a,' but perhaps the object 'b' ... Why not, he responded, pointing out the extreme difficulty ...."[81] It is precisely this investigation Deleuze and Guattari would embark on in *Anti-Oedipus* in 1972. As Deleuze writes, *das Ding*, the Thing, was not to be understood as constitutive of an isolated subject, but as the Real of "a social body serving as a basis for latent potentialities"[82] that make up the subject. Without going any further in the theoretical exposition of this approach, we shall confine ourselves here to drawing from it a few consequences for analytic technique.[83]

By revealing the real object, the support of the phantasy and the cause of desire, it becomes possible to perform the analysis of the "deceitful outlooks" [*fausses fenêtres*, false windows] of group fantasies:

we will need to decode those phenomena that encourage the group to withdraw into itself: leaderships, identifications, effects of suggestion, disavowals, scapegoating, and so forth. We will also need to decode anything that tends to promote local laws and idiosyncratic formations involving interdictions, rites, and anything else that tends to protect the group by buttressing it against signifying storms in which as the result of a specific operation of misrecognition—the threat is experienced as issuing from the outside. This has the effect of producing those deceitful outlooks peculiar to group delusions [*fantasmes*].[84]

Based on this true journey through group phantasies, the subject can free itself from the subjugated group in favor of a new type of group where its speech becomes, on the contrary, constitutive. Guattari describes it as follows: "Thus one belongs to such a group not so as to hide from desire and death, engaging in a collective process of neurotic obsession, but owing to a particular problem which is ultimately not eternal in nature, but transitory. This is what I have called the structure of 'transversality.'"[85] As opposed to subjugated groups such as religious groups, here we observe the agnostic dynamic that makes up the subject groups: The Other constituted by the group is no longer absolutized. This is precisely what gives subject groups greater possibilities for overcoming individual symptomatic impasses, and for the emergence of a non-subjugated subjectivity. The subject can confront its desire in the experience of the group itself, it can speak about its desire rather than being spoken by it, "gain access to the group's inwardness and interpret it" rather than manifest it.[86] The subject can critique its desire without being negated by it.

In conclusion, if the subjugated groups can be modified, if subjective and unconscious subjugation can be analyzed—and partially removed—by the analysis of phantasies, the social situation and its subject can also change. The subjugated group is given its law from the outside and "one can always count on finding refuge in the group's structures of misrecognition."[87] But "from the moment the group becomes a subject of its own destiny and assumes its own finitude and death, it is then that the data received by the superego is modified, and, consequently, the threshold of the castration complex, specific to a given social order, can be locally modified."[88] The "set[ing] in motion" of "a [new] type of castration complex" linked to "different social demands" loosens the superego's grip: one "accept[s] being 'put on trial,' being verbally laid bare by others, [and] a certain type of reciprocal challenge, and humor" emerges.[89] In other words, it is not the phantasy's fate to founder in the subjugated group's impasse. On the contrary, there is only subjugation through lack of analysis. We can wager that this perspective has the elements of an essential *modus operandi* for any truly revolutionary future practice. In any case, this is what the members of CERFI (Center for Studies, Research, and Institutional Training) explicitly attempted at the La Borde clinic by trying to interpret reflexively their modes of action, struggle, and intervention on site.[90]

6
Revival of Revolutionary Psychoanalysis in Germany: The Heidelberg Experiment

At the end of the 1960s, a politically engaged psychoanalytic theory and practice emerged within German psychiatry. The experiment took place in Heidelberg. As with the French movement, its commitment to revolutionary Marxism reflected a desire to continue the postwar fight for emancipation. But in West Germany, such a program meant that activists at the time had to confront the specter of the Third Reich that still haunted Germany. The Nazi bureaucracy had set up a systematic campaign to murder mentally and physically ill people, which prefigured the mass murder of Jews.[1] And we know today that the principle middle managers of the Nazi regime's institutions were reinstated after the war under the pretext of the anticommunist struggle without any real concern.[2] That was precisely the case for academic psychiatry in Heidelberg, where several doctors who had participated in Nazi crimes of euthanasia were still on the job. At the end of the 1960s, at least four caregivers were former SS.[3] This may partly explain why the Heidelberg Sozialistisches Patientenkolletiv (SPK)—the "Socialist Patient Collective"—was far more harshly repressed than any similar attempts in other

European countries. Its members suffered imprisonment and torture.[4]

But we can also ask, along with Guattari, whether the violence and relentlessness of the German authorities against the SPK were not simply proportional to their fear of seeing the critical coherence and political scope of the Heidelberg collective spread rapidly:

> Something completely new took place, a move away from ideology towards a genuine political struggle. For the first time, the psychiatric struggle went into the streets, the neighborhoods, and the entire city. Like the 22 March Movement at Nanterre, the SPK mobilized for a real struggle, and the repression knew it![5]

A good enough reason to be interested today in the experiment of the SPK, which is still little known.

The Political Context of the SPK's Birth

The collective formed at the very end of the 1960s in a general inpatient psychiatric ward at the Heidelberg University policlinic. It brought together patients and doctors under the impetus of Dr. Huber. Huber, born into a family of modest means, grew up in a small village in the south of West Germany. He financed his education by working in a factory, and with a scholarship, then began his career in 1964 as an assistant to Professor Walter von Baeyer in Heidelberg. As soon as he arrived at the policlinic, Huber worked with Dr. Spazier to build a student counseling center based on the fact that the number of student patients had risen sharply: from 85 in 1964, to 200 in 1968. Sensitive to young people's distress, he sympathized with their cause and took part in demonstrations, militant conferences, and critical working groups at the university.

Although still haunted by the specter of Nazism, which remained a taboo subject, the university was at the time the scene of an intense reform, notably under the impetus of Professor von Baeyer, who had been breathing new life into psychiatry for a decade or so. As in most European countries, progressive changes were under way in Heidelberg: The clinic had been opened up, the gates removed, and separate male and female quarters abolished. But the old power remained firmly rooted: According to Christian Pross, the author of a monograph on the SPK, two

Figure 7 In the SPK group meeting room, September/October 1970. Wolfgang Huber is in the center with a cigarette (copyright BPK, Berlin, Dist. RMN-Grand Palais/Image BPK/Digne Meller Marcovicz)

types of psychiatry coexisted in conflict then. The student revolts of the 1960s precipitated and crystallized this unresolved conflict, particularly around the SPK.

Huber quickly found himself in charge of the vast majority of the policlinic's patients. He attempted to put into practice a new therapeutics that was critical of psychiatric power. This included, among other things, reducing the distance between patient and caregiver, but also unmasking the ideology of health under which psychiatry operated. To this end, the SPK claimed continuity with the theories put into practice by Wilhelm Reich and drew inspiration from anti-psychiatry. Having diagnosed the failure of the proletarian movement, the collective sought to extend the reach of Marxian analysis to domains it had hitherto neglected, and which were essential according to its members for the realization of any revolutionary project: The goal was to push Marxist theory further through Freudian contributions.

The Theoretical Constellation of the SPK

Marx had shown that workers, forced to sell their labor power, were thereby dispossessed of the product of their labor and alienated into social relations that appeared to them as objective relations between things. He observed that, under capitalism, products of labor were transformed into commodities and presented to the worker as though they were autonomous. They took on a mystical character that did not result from their use value, but from their commodity form. This process, which he called "commodity fetishism," resulted in the worker's "false consciousness," which attributed to products of labor qualities that they did not have, which masked the reality of human relations of domination and exploitation.

In the political ferment of the 1960s and 1970s, Marx's theory of commodity fetishism aroused new interest, even in analytic circles. In France, Lacan referred to it and even gave it priority over Freud's theory of fetishism. He noted that surplus value is first and foremost a "plus-de-jouir" [surplus enjoyment/no more enjoyment].[6] Though unlike Reich he did not claim to do so; Lacan thereby displaced the question of the Marxist concept of alienation as well as of "false consciousness" into a field that both goes beyond these concepts and enlightens them in return: the field of the relationships between the unconscious and *jouissance*. This problem was also addressed by Guattari, who developed his argument based on his comparative reading of Lacan—whose disciple he still was—and of Reich. Finally, we must note that these theoretical elaborations among analysts occurred during an intense political period, marked in most European countries by the "sexual revolution" and the revival of revolutionary political movements among the youth and workers. The rediscovery of Reich's work at this very particular historical conjuncture at the end of the 1960s—which resonated in many ways with the 1920s and 1930s and the first failed sexual and political revolution—was anything but a coincidence.

Remember, in the 1930s, Reich politicized the sexual issue with the objective of preventing the masses from sinking into Nazism, so that they could carry out their revolution—the communist revolution. More generally, he came to the idea that sexual life must be politicized because the alienation that struck the masses in fact touched on a thousand and one aspects of their intimate, ordinary lives. Simply describing in theory the capitalist exploitation of labor for which they paid the price did not allow for the ("class") consciousness necessary to accomplish the revolution. Furthermore, Reich had made a critique of Stalin's regression and shown that a revolution that declared itself communist could turn into its opposite. From this point of view, Nazism and Stalinism, like the bourgeois capitalist model, shared many common reactionary features, beyond their undeniable differences, which kept the masses under domination. In the revolutionary perspective sharpened by psychoanalysis, the goal was not only to reclaim the products of labor but also to break with the commodity and contractual relations that pegged them to the capitalist *jouissance* made of false needs.[7] For even when it wasn't at work, the subject's real needs were diverted to ersatz desires that reinforced the process of domination. Hence, the Marxist concept alone was not enough to explain the process of alienation it set out to describe—and to undo. From their specific point of view, the analyst could shed light on the psychological operations of commodity fetishism and its false consciousness. They could also indicate the psychoanalytic ways and means by which it was possible to be emancipated from them. During a time of protest and political awakening in the 1960s and 1970s in Germany, Wilhelm Reich emerged from oblivion. As in France, his ideas were circulated once again. In a way, the SPK aimed to continue Reich's program of the politicization of daily life from the collective's own place: medicine.

Reich among the Doctors

The SPK did not take on a single perspective of critiquing psychiatry or practicing antipsychiatry, but more generally, of politicizing, in the Reichian tradition, the issue of illness beyond mere psychiatry. During the 1970s, its ambition distinguished it from other attempts that did not have the same political effects of revolutionary contagion. This radical direction was defended in a manifesto with the title *Turn Illness into a Weapon*, published in France in 1973 by publisher Champ Libre—which also translated a book by Reich during the same time. The same text had been circulating since 1972 as a pamphlet, in German and in French, with a preface by Jean-Paul Sartre. There, Sartre presented the SPK's argument as a simple homology between social alienation and mental illness. Though he defended the SPK's political project, he still remained hostile to psychoanalysis, and did not see the radicality and the psychoanalytical-political edge of the collective. He considered their position as just another "radicalized anti-psychiatry." But the originality of the SPK's conception lies in the fact that it exceeds both psychiatry and anti-psychiatry, and that it defends the thesis that the essential process of alienation is rooted in illness in general, as well as in the medicine that is supposed to treat it.

The SPK thus carried political critique much further than classical Marxist analysis. The real sites of the production of alienation are to be found where we thought we were only dealing with pure organic causality and with a science—medicine—that was a priori non-political. Counterintuitive and radical, this argument threw new light on sectors of society that could seem to be completely neutral, outside the *polis*. How is medical science, which treats illnesses people suffer in their bodies, political? By radically questioning medicine and its systems, health and its ideology, illness and its symptoms, the SPK showed that, on the contrary, these are privileged domains to attack with a materialist critique deepened by psychoanalytic input: "In the SPK, in the aftermath of this Reichian beginning and its historical-materialistic reprocessing, illness was understood as the contradiction within life, as the in-itself broken life."[8] A new field of investigation opened up, relating to a *politics of sick bodies*.

The SPK drew in particular on the work of Frantz Fanon. During the Algerian liberation struggle, he noticed the disappearance among his formerly colonized patients of both their psychiatric symptoms and their somatic ones, like ulcers or deformities of the spinal column.[9] These cases Fanon describes of subjects whose bodies betrayed symptoms of colonial political repression were paradigmatic for the SPK. Beyond "mental illness" alone, it seemed that all illness and its symptoms were inextricably linked to the capitalist system. Thus, any doctor, and more generally anyone "seriously concerned with symptoms of illness has to deal with the power of capitalist society."[10] The SPK stood in direct opposition to the neutrality of medical science. Before being an organic fact, illness and its symptoms are a political fact, even the political fact par excellence. We thus need to reconsider the very conception of health in a capitalist regime and explain how and why medical professionals and patients alike overlooked the process of political alienation to which they are subjected. But before we get to that, we will see that Fanon's radical clinical findings, taken up by the SPK, find an explanation in the Marxist concept of the drives as Reich had proposed.

Partial Drive, Exchange Value, and Illness

> The behavior of the individual in this way is determined by sado-masochistic tendencies, neurotic anxiety, leader-specific identification processes and perseveration tendencies (obsessions). This is understood by Reich as the sexualization of non-genital instinct impulses which for their part have reciprocal effects that already get impeded in the early childhood development of the level of genital stimuli in favor of oral satisfaction tendencies and anal-fixation behaviors.[11]

For the SPK, as for Reich, capital's effectiveness on its subjects derives from a libidinal diversion brought about by education and certain bourgeois institutions, to which the SPK added the healthcare system, giving it decisive precedence. Reich had indeed shown in *The Invasion of Compulsory Sex-Morality* that the emergence and consolidation of the capitalist mode of production presupposes a specific transformation of the libido.[12] The capture and exploitation of productive forces, as well as the realization of a purpose of unlimited accumulation, cannot emerge historically without profound upheavals in sexual economy. Reich established its genesis and functioning. For him, capitalism's libidinal economy consists in preventing subjects from realizing genitality and orgasmic power (such as is seen at work in traditional non-capitalist societies like the Trobriand people)[13] and maintaining them in an economy of partial drives. The SPK takes up the idea that capital is supported by this economy of the drives and offers a description of it: "Gender specific characteristics inclusive of biological make-up as well as the structure of individual perception, are determined through the sexualization of the partial drives whose activation is the result of the competition between economic and repressed genital tendencies."[14]

Here social repression in the interest of economic forces finds its mode of transmission [trouve sa courroie de transmission] in the repression of the subject's genitality. The hypothesis that capital operates by cutting into the very material of the subject's libido, intervening directly on the unconscious, allows us to rethink the concept of alienation by specifying its clinical drivers [ressorts]. The operation of capturing the subject would then take place on two levels. On the one hand, the energy from which the economy draws its strength originates in repression. Repression, far from being reduced to intrapsychic mechanisms, is the engine through which it grows its empire. On the other hand, if the libido is diverted from its genital destiny and the pathways of sublimation blocked, libidinal expression falls under the domination of partial drives, which capital works with to shape the subject according to its interests. Thus desire, diverted into ersatz desires for the profit of capital, can be integrated into the fetishistic circuit of the commodity, and the choices the subject believes it is making become libidinally overdetermined. The economy of partial drives also explains why the subject remains ideologically subjugated—because the subject itself desires it. Marx's "false consciousness" would thus be built, more profoundly than he intended, on a diversion of desire, and the driver of alienation would be sexual.

Marx's theory of fetishism is revised and deepened by the input of psychoanalysis. Social relations become alienated from the subject's true needs and end up appearing to the subject as things because they are libidinally overdetermined by capital. The primacy of exchange value over use value would also fall under the libidinal economy. Indeed, for the SPK, "partial drives" are the "*material realization* of the rule of exchange-value in the individual."[15] A radical thesis that establishes the importance of the sexual within the economic clarifies the idea that relationships maintained between subjects become, under capitalism, object-to-object relationships: "Through the total subordination of all life to exchange value, relations 'among people' are determined as relations among objects."[16]

However, capital's libidinal appropriation of the subject presents the SPK with a major and decisive contradiction. Indeed, such a hold on the subject thwarts the normal development of sexuality and ultimately negates it: "The complete fragmentation of sexual energies through the capitalist relations of production into partial drives (voyeurism, object fetishism, perversion, etc.) is the simple negation of sexuality."[17] This negation of sexuality is central because it designates the real expropriation carried out by capital, while at the same time identifying it clinically. To divert the libido to its benefit, capital must constrain its subjects' sexuality and place it in its service. By playing on the drives, it seeks to exploit its proletarian subject further. But by blocking the libidinal flow, it tears its subject to pieces, with deadly effects. Maintained in an unsatisfying libidinal economy, the dislocated subject will sooner or later fall ill. Turning individual needs into false freedom and commodities proves costly—and even fatal—in the more or less long term. Its corollary is the triggering of symptoms: "But the individual's need for life contradicts capital's need for surplus value; the symptom is the immediately sensually perceptible unity of this contradiction."[18] More precisely, by capturing the subject for the necessities of production, capital inhibits what the subject might protest against (the SPK identifies this protest as the possibly progressive moment of illness). The blocked libidinal expression transforms sooner or later into violence against the subject. Distracted from the reality of this process by "false objects," based on "false desires," the subject soon feels the effects. These "emotional failures," which cannot be symbolized, result in "stomach pains, gall stones, circulatory problems, kidney stones, cramps of all kinds, into impotence, head colds, toothaches, skin diseases ... asthma, ... in psychosis, etc."[19] The "contradiction" has literally taken over the subject's body and the symptom is its "immediately sensually perceptible unity." For the SPK, life under capitalism turns against itself and "breaks down."

Capital's contradiction is that it negates that from which it draws its force: It makes ill the very person it needs to make its profit. This point is essential from the SPK's revolutionary perspective. If illness is produced by capital, it cannot tolerate the process being unmasked. But neither can it tolerate accumulation being threatened by the physical and mental exhaustion of the subjects it exploits. Hence the ideological task that, according to the SPK, is the responsibility of the healthcare system: masking the fact that working in a capitalist regime makes you ill.

Political Critique of the Healthcare System as Ideological Apparatus

The SPK thus develops a political critique of the healthcare system as an ideological state apparatus. To do so, they draw from—and radicalize—contemporary analyses by Jean-Claude Polack, a psychoanalyst at La Borde. He had shown that capitalist medicine does not respond to a "demand for care," but proceeds by breaking down "health needs" into those whose satisfaction fits within the logic of capital accumulation.[20] The SPK was particularly interested in the doctor–patient relationship:

> In the case of doctor–patient relationships, e.g., each of the two partners in the relationship is an object of the same subject, of capital. The patient, as the object of the apparent subject, puts his psychological suffering and his need for change in the hand of the doctor, according to plan, who becomes a caretaker of capital like he is also a caretaker of sickness.[21]

Objects of the same subject—capital—the doctor and patient thus constitute a matrix for the process of capitalist alienation. The ideological construction of the individual as sick person occurs at the heart of the relationship maintained between the two. Bedridden, wearing a hospital gown, the subject becomes a patient, and the doctor will be able to proceed with material and bureaucratic treatment of the illness. It is analyzed "chemically and radiologically ... pharmaceutically, electrically, radioactively, surgically treated," and so on.[22] All of these objective technical operations dispossess the subject, who is "confirmed in the negative aspect of their illness" (78): "The individual, in his illness and status as patient, acutely experiences his role as a pure object through his defenselessness, isolation, and loss of rights."[23]

Even more than in the wage relationship, where the worker retains their labor power and some rights (in their bourgeois contractual form), in the healthcare system the subject is alone and no longer really possesses anything. They are no longer even a "subject with rights," as the reality of psychiatric institutions frequently demonstrates. But it is precisely here that the subject's condition is revealed in its naked truth, as "pure object of capital." In fact, the alienation of the imaginary is at its most complete here, since the doctor–patient relationship aims to create the patient's "need for treatment," right down to their desire for healing: "With his need for treatment his inability to act becomes a certainty."[24] Illness and its treatment reveal the "fetishism of health," a powerful motive leading to the subject's acquiescence to its own submission by producing its desire to heal. The subject is dispossessed of their own will and a reliance on official medicine to be healed is created. The "success of the 'treatment'" thus takes on a new meaning:

It essentially consists in producing the desired transformation—including by the patient—by subjectivizing them in the figure of "healing." The true nature and function of treatment thereby remain hidden from the eyes of its principal actors. For, in reality, "successful treatment" corresponds in fact and in substance with "reproduction of the sick person's employability, of his ability to function in [the anti-human, illness-engendering] social production process of capital, in his 'rehabilitation.'"[25] For the SPK, the "doctor–patient relationship [is] defined by the entire health care system" and in it "capital and state maintain a state-of-the-art instrument of oppression."[26] The doctor's aim is to produce "for capital [...] newly exploitable labor power, according to orders."[27] We must therefore reconsider health itself as a *curbed* illness (or, if you like, a less severe illness), concealing the relations of production that, by structural necessity, make people sick. The real function of healthcare systems is to manage and absorb crises of capital, as much as to facilitate its reproduction within acceptable limits—including countering its totalitarian tendency towards the outright elimination of sick people, as practiced by the Nazis, for example:

> The health care system has on the one hand the task of raising the norm, and on the other hand of selecting that labor power which no longer corresponds to the norm and preserving it at the least possible cost—or of liquidating it outright and euthanizing outsiders, as in the Third Reich. To be healthy, therefore, means to be exploitable.[28]

Such a perspective obviously renders obsolete the idea that there could be a specific "workplace medicine." As Jean-Claude Polack writes, cited by the SPK: "It's no joke to speak of workplace medicine; our society knows no other. All medicine is the regulation of the capacity to work. The work norm shapes the judgment of the doctor with a standard which is more precise than measures of biological or physiological value."[29] The SPK's chilling conclusion is that illness is "the only form of 'life' possible under capitalism" (8) and that its suppression is impossible since health consists in "the ability to continue to produce while still ill" [translation modified]. The worker's condition would thus be a crippled product.[30]

Patient Power and Proletarian Power

From the SPK's conclusions, it also follows that illness is the true inner limit of capitalism: "However, capitalism produces, in the form of illness, the most dangerous threat to itself [...] *Objectively*, illness, as defective (= not exploitable) labor power, is the gravedigger of capitalism."[31]

For if everyone was seriously ill and incapable of working, there would be no one left to produce surplus value. We can then understand that, for the SPK, illness in overdeveloped countries becomes the revolutionary category par excellence: "objectively, because surplus value can only be extracted through the exploitation of human labor power"[32]—but also because this exploitation can only lead to the impoverishment of the masses and the intensification of illness. And so it is under its concrete determination that the proletariat must find the means to make revolution. Indeed, subjectively, illness does not just cause inhibition in the subject but also the possibility of protest. Remember that the symptom is "the appearance of the essence of illness as protest and the hindrance of protest."[33] But it remains possible to liberate libidinal energy that the sick subject produces in the solipsism of its symptom by freeing and using the "progressive moment of illness, i.e. protest":[34] "repression of protest, which is indicated by symptoms of illness, is resolved in the dialectic of individual and society; from the repressed feelings of the sick (of those who consciously suffer) the energies of action will be set free and the explosives activated that will smash the controlling system of permanent murder."[35]

A new collective structure capturing the liberated energy materializes the lifting of the inhibition that is maintained and produced by capital and its apparatuses: the socialist patient collective. Returned to its genital destiny, the drive allows men and women to rediscover their desire and their consciousness, and to transform "object–object relations into subject–subject relations": "As a collectively conscious process, illness is the revolutionary productive force, according to the level of its effectiveness: limited protest, conscious protest, collective consciousness, struggle in solidarity."[36]

To be successful, this movement must, at least temporarily, be supported by the figure of the doctor. In their patients' real interest, the doctor must also work towards the liberation of the protest contained in the illness:

> Once illness is recognized as the starting point and the end result of the capitalist process of production, then

> the progressive activity of doctors can consist only in striving to eliminate their capital-oriented function which is inimical to patients and to life. They must strive for the transformation of this society and not, for instance—as it is practiced and misunderstood in its crippled form—in the production of patients' "health" and thereby in the temporary elimination of the need for "treatment" by each individual patient.[37]

More broadly, the SPK defends a subversion of the medical function. New medical science must serve "the patients." In fact, the aim is to socialize "the means of scientific production for and through the people":[38]

> The progressive turn of the doctor's function can only be practiced by working in solidarity together with the patient. The essential moment of this praxis is the socialization of the doctor's function. That means concretely the socialization of the special knowledge and experience of the doctor and not their transmission according to the authority structures of education and training programs. The recognition of the object role which the patient and doctor have in common presents the foundation on which this socialization process, oriented on the thing in common, is completed.[39]

This process is thus a "reciprocal" "collective learning process,"[40] in which the doctor and patient are transformed by their common practice. Here the SPK goes beyond the various psychiatric reformisms. As Guattari recalls, the SPK's political project was not about defending the rights of "poor patients," nor only "giving patients freedom."[41] It was not a matter of decompartmentalizing authorities and sharing knowledge (that the psychiatrists could talk with nurses[42] or that the caregivers and patients could talk with each other, like in the "therapeutic communities"[43]). In Heidelberg, "everything that was done, everything that was decided, it was always by the patients themselves."[44]

This fundamental break is all the more clear-cut given that the SPK's concept of illness is extensive. The collective spread quickly and, based on "a small in-hospital experiment," soon envisioned "mass struggle." Their fight extended beyond the hospital, and their numbers grew from a few dozen to hundreds of members. According to Guattari, things were "set to go even further," if the collective had not been brutally repressed. Indeed, by maintaining that "illness is the truth of the subject," the SPK took it to a universal dimension. It concerns everyone: The patient is not only the one who is identified as such by the hospital. We have seen that confining the patient to the hospital was an illusion. Rather, the hospital patient, because they no longer have anything (neither labor force or rights), exposes the process of alienation and dispossession out in the open. Reduced by capital to a pure object, the patient also reveals an internal limit.

What are the political consequences of the SPK's theories? First and foremost, they bring down the ideological barrier between the "ill" and the "well," and they furnish revolutionary action with a new preferred space in "care" sites. The whole medical fiction of a separation between normal and pathological ends up collapsing, along with its apparatus, to the benefit of the collective, which puts into practice objective solidarity between all exploited subjects. Through this collective, the very idea that every subject has of illness and the sick person, and its relationship with them, changes. From this point of view, the collective that emerges truly enables us to put into practice a different mode of being together.

To describe this subjective and material movement, the SPK speak of "multifocal expansionism": Labelled as sick, each subject is a crystallization of social contradictions. The patient collective helps to channel and precipitate these contradictions. The subject is no longer alien to them, like under the regime of the division of medical labor, it gradually comes out of its isolation:

> Each sick person is a focus in specific ways. Objectively, each sick person is the burn point of social contradictions. In the process of the conscious development of the contradictions of repression and protest contained in illness, the quality of "focus" as the burn point of social relations (contradictions) become a subjective quality, that is the sick person is someone conscious of his suffering and of social relations, of an objective and subjective focus.[45]

Through a conscious process of reappropriation of what they were unconsciously deprived of, the sick person is led by the group to emancipate themselves. Then they can become home to a new mode of being and of consciousness. By freeing the progressive moment of protest, the SPK seeks to restore the subject's power to act: "The process of transcending the quality of 'burn point' (limitation) into the quality of 'flame' is the emancipation of the object, the person being treated, into becoming a subject, an *acting agent*, through cooperation and solidarity."[46]

The collective's practice attests to a more global movement that exceeds psychiatry and that can be described philosophically as a movement from the object towards the subject:

> Only cooperation with others in solidarity makes the transition from object to subject possible. This means that the many isolated objects of social relationships can become subjects only through collective praxis on the basis of cooperative solidarity. In this way the individuals cooperating together have changed for themselves the social relations of which they constitute a part: and simply because they are now collectively—no longer only as individuals—part of social relations [...] Together in the collective they become as far as possible and to some degree actually, that is effectively, their own subject.[47]

This is why Guattari sees the Heidelberg experiment as "the psychiatric equivalent of the Paris Commune in terms of proletarian struggles."[48] From this point of view, the virulent reaction it provoked from the German authorities rings out like a repetition of history.

Repression

The activity of the SPK and Dr. Huber rapidly caused a disturbance. In 1970, Huber's contract was not renewed;

patients and students mobilized to keep him on. On July 6, 1970, 25 patients along with Huber occupied the university's management offices. They called for patients to have control over health insurance, the clinic's internal rules and budget, as well as the independence of public health from industry and the military. They also demanded the provision of a house with at least ten rooms for the treatment of the most vulnerable, with university funding and therapeutic equipment. The collective obtained formal recognition of its existence by the university.

But the Federal Ministry of Education intervened to ensure that the university cease all negotiations with the SPK. On September 18, 1970, the ministry planned to issue a decree for the SPK's evacuation of the premises. In reaction, the collective sought support from political, media, and religious figures to ward off the threat and buy some time. Most of the people contacted declined. Only the prestigious magazine *Der Spiegel* published a relatively sympathetic article at the beginning of October. However, the SPK's power of attraction was in full swing: in July 1970, the collective had between 150 and 200 patients. Between 40 and 50 people were permanently on the SPK's premises, considered by many patients to be a warm and welcoming place.[49]

At the beginning of the summer of 1971, the collective was the target of disproportionate repression, and the repercussions were felt beyond borders. An international group formed by patients, healthcare staff, psychiatrists, and psychoanalysts came from Holland, France, Italy, and Germany to conduct an on-site investigation with unequivocal conclusions:

In a closed-door meeting, the University Senate decided to resort to the law enforcement. Pretext was provided in July 1971 by an exchange of gunfire in the vicinity of Heidelberg. Blaming it on the SPK meant it could be brought down by the most brutal means. Three hundred cops armed with machine guns forced their way onto the SPK's premises, helicopters were flying overhead, the *Bundesgrenzschutz* (Federal Border Guard) was mobilized, searches were conducted without warrant, Dr. Huber's children taken hostage, patients and doctors arrested, the accused drugged to force them to cooperate.[50]

At the time of the trial in 1972, Deleuze and Guattari traveled to Heidelberg to support the SPK.[51] Despite international pressure, Huber and one of his relatives were sentenced to four and a half years in prison for participation in a criminal organization, a particularly heavy sentence. A second trial took place in May 1973, then a third in 1974. The resistance was organized and growing. A call for solidarity with the defendants was issued. During a psychoanalytic conference in Milan in 1975—whose theme was sexuality and politics[52]—2,000 endorsed the call. The next month, Sartre, de Beauvoir, Basaglia, Foucault, Cooper, Castel, Gentis, Guattari, and many other figures signed a press release denouncing the repression against the SPK.[53] It was also an opportunity to take stock of the collective's activities, theoretical developments, and clinical successes, as reported in *Recherches*, a magazine close to La Borde:

> During the SPK's existence, therapeutic work had progressed to such an extent that within a year and a half 500 patients could join the collective and it was possible to welcome a further 500. This was made possible by overcoming the traditional separation between patients and healthcare staff (including doctors) and giving way to new forms of therapy where the individual's problems were examined collectively [...] The group took its weakest member's problems as its starting point and oriented itself according to their needs.[54]

In theorizing its own practice, the Heidelberg collective did not claim to be a vanguard. It was clear to the SPK that multifocal expansionism could occur anywhere. Since the proletariat was still determined by it, by turning illness into a weapon, they could become truly revolutionary.

Conclusion:
For Another Psychoanalysis

What critical insights for today's analysis can we draw from this (too) brief history? As early as the end of the 1980s, Russell Jacoby observed that American psychoanalysis was struck by a real repression: "Even the appropriate vocabulary—'left-wing Freudians,' 'Marxist psychoanalysts,' 'political psychoanalysts,' even 'humanism' itself—sticks in the throat of contemporary psychoanalysis."[1] However, these are terms that apply to the main actors in this history. But we have to admit that the same is true, if not worse, for psychoanalysis in France today ... Abstracting its practice from its sociohistoric specificity and its clinical and theoretical implications, it relegates to the shadows crucial aspects of the discipline's history, which we have tried to restore to their rightful place.

We have seen that defining psychoanalysis as apolitical, neutral, indifferentist, and pessimistic has not been without consequences. Beyond the clinical issues at stake, the very possibility of a political reading of its history has been abolished. In this respect, the psychoanalism of the 1980s proved particularly consistent, applying the same contempt for history and its revolutionary moments as to the history of the discipline itself ... albeit perhaps with even more rage. The critique of psychoanalism is therefore all the more inseparable from a project of a people's history of psychoanalysis, precisely because psychoanalism has always denied this history. Writing this progressive history thus reveals the reifying operations of the disciplinary history on which it is based. The critique of 1980s psychoanalism finally allows us to bring out a clearly positive point of view *for psychoanalysis*, and to reconnect with its revolutionary tradition. Hence, isn't it history itself that makes itself heard and regains its rights? Whatever one may say, Freud would probably not have been surprised by the psychoanalytic movement around May 1968, and, on the contrary, it is rather the promotion of "indifferentism" in analysis that must now be questioned and regarded as dubious.

The thesis of Freud's alleged "indifferentism" is supported, as we have seen, by a statement Ernest Jones attributed to him: This point is not indifferent when we know Jones's role in the history of the movement. Not only because Freud's own position cannot be reduced to this but also because this approach disregards the project of achieving a politics of "social justice" that analysts pursued during certain fruitful periods in the history of psychoanalysis. Jones is the one who "adapted" psychoanalysis to the Nazi regime, and he actively contributed to driving the most politically committed psychoanalysts, and Jews, too, from their positions. However, this dark period in the history of psychoanalysis and the transformation of the "Berlin policlinic" into the "Göring Institute" remains little known—and Jones's position in the analytic field is rarely questioned. But an article by Elisabeth Brainin and Isidor Kaminer led the way,[2] suggesting that the denial of this turbulent time has had unidentified effects on analytic institutions and analysts themselves in their clinical practice. Thus it is worth re-reading the history of our discipline over and against the story promoted by certain hegemonic psychoanalytic circles in France. And rather than cheaply pointing to Reich's supposed excesses during this period, we must shed light on Jones's excesses, which take a less respectable turn here than usual. It is no accident that Reich's expulsion from the IPA in 1933 is so often highlighted by the dogma. Yet it was not done for the reasons given: Wilhelm Reich was not primarily kicked out over a theoretical dispute, or because he strayed into the field of politics, nor even because he was crazy as some go so far to claim. The legend of Reich's expulsion for his "personal excesses" is used to hide the major political blindness of the IPA and its new direction, which he denounced. For the affiliation of the German Psychoanalytic Society with new Nazi Party institutions relied precisely on the argument of psychoanalysis's neutrality, at the same time that Jews and Reds were driven out of the psychoanalytic institution. Soon psychoanalysis itself would participate in its own expulsion inside the Göring Institute.

Today's defenders of "psychoanalytic neutrality" and Reich's detractors should ponder this lesson: The "rescue of psychoanalysis" by Jones, IPA president, actually precipitated its shipwreck within the Third Reich. Whether they like it or not, their arguments are inextricably linked to this historic period of compromise and to this argumentative structure, which is pure sophistry. And for those in contemporary analytic circles who still claim to be "rescuing psychoanalysis," this phrase reveals its dark side: the side borne by Jones's disastrous party line, supported by Freud in the 1930s.

Finally, a word must be said about Freudian pessimism, which is often used to cover the whole of his work and guide its reading, and to ignore the moment when Freud was in favor of the communist endeavor, optimistic about the political future, and committed to a people's clinic in the city. It is therefore no accident that Jones's biography of Freud remains a reference for many contemporary French analysts: it may well be that the French neo-psychoanalysis is Jonesian. The triumph of Jones's "backroom deals" to (re)write the analytic movement's history has hindered the epistemological possibility of appreciating the politically engaged praxis that animated most of the interwar analysts, among whom Reich's name is really only the "emergent signifier." And it is the same process—truly just rendering down—that contemporary psychoanalism is carrying out with Guattari to deal with the 1960s and 1970s, and more generally to dismiss any attempt at progressive psychoanalysis. Psychoanalism subjects Guattari's name, symbolic of a revolutionary moment, to the same delegitimization procedure as Reich's, thus extending Jones's move. These figures are then hijacked and assigned a new function, a condition of this reactionary epistemology that presents them as marginal, excessive, even crazy, and finally disreputable. Our discipline's progressive history is erased, and psychoanalism can thus overshadow the multitude of names of those who shared the same fight. Taking up such a revisionist strategy deprives the discipline of its history.

But the mythical and deadly days of a supposedly purified psychoanalysis are certainly over. May this book be its harbinger and arouse the desire of other psychoanalytic researchers to continue down this uncharted path. Many psychoanalytic experiences await in the shadows. May we rediscover their light to illuminate our present. After the war, especially in the United States (in Topeka under Menninger's influence, and in Chicago under Franz Alexander's influence) free outpatient clinics on Berlin's model were created. Fenichel, in Topeka during his American exile, recalls finding there an atmosphere comparable to Berlin's and Prague's. During his exile, Bernfeld also created a Free Institute of Psychoanalysis on the Berlin model in San Francisco. Erich Fromm and Frieda Fromm-Reichmann, psychoanalysts who had founded the Frankfurt Institute of Psychoanalysis in the 1920s, continued their experiment at Chestnut Lodge, in Maryland. We should also mention the experiments carried out in Algeria at the Bilda Hospital around Frantz Fanon, as well as those in England that led to anti-psychiatry from Laing, Berke, and Cooper to Kingsley Hall, to the exemplary analytic treatments, like with Mary Barnes; or even, in 1970s Italy, the experiment of the Consultorio Populare di Niguarda, as well those carried out in France from Mannoni to Bonneuil and those, following the "Lander" group, from the Psychoanalytic Laboratory at Vincennes. The list actually turns out to be quite long, without even mentioning the most recent contemporary attempts and those currently underway. These few examples are but a summary of a living international history that remains to be written. We therefore hope that the necessarily partial choice that we have had to make still contributes in liberating research in these still little-known areas, and will act as an invitation to continue and to deepen the perspective of *psychoanalytic political studies* [in English]. May this *living* multitude, from which we have been cut off, resurface in the present to liberate us from the mortification of psychoanalism. May this book contribute to opening new paths of research and encourage today's—and tomorrow's—militant analysts to engage in clinical work with the contemporary working classes, as promoted during a relatively long and fertile period by the father of psychoanalysis himself.

Notes

Introduction

1. But this did not make Freud a communist.
2. Russel Jacoby, *The Repression of Psychoanalysis: Otto Fenichel and the Political Freudians* (New York: Basic Books, 1983).
3. Even if it is true that this political engagement was more pronounced than that of previous generations, and was not without its differences of opinion and generational conflict, to which we will return, the fact remains that *basically everyone*, old or young, was politically engaged.
4. With Jung, we aren't dealing at this point with psychoanalysis at all.
5. Though I do not follow her career beyond this point, it must be noted that she continued her political engagement in an analytic practice with the revolutionaries in Managua.
6. Of course, I am aware of the gaps in my brief presentation, which could have focused on many other psychoanalytic figures and experiments that have been ignored or relegated to the background. I will return to this in the conclusion.
7. Though I'm not a historian by training, I was pushed towards this investigation first and foremost by concerns in the field of clinical analytic practice (see my previous book, *L'héritage*). But I am inclined to think, following the example of experienced historians, that it is this very contingency, and the assumed bias that stems from it, which gives my words strength and makes them intelligible. A piece of writing always has its position, and the minimal

rigor of the researcher, far from consisting in pretending to be abstracted from it in the name of "objectivity," is to recognize their bias, which in this case, it will be understood, is towards that of the primacy of the *revolutionary perspective in psychoanalysis*.

8. Frantz Fanon, *Wretched of the Earth*, trans. Richard Philcox (New York: Grove Press, [1963] 2004).

9. Marcel Gauchet, "Débat autour de *L'homme sans gravité* avec Pierre Beckouche," December 2002, in Charles Melman, *La nouvelle économie psychique* (Toulouse: Érès, 2010).

10. "If our anthropologists and sociologists wanted to get serious, instead of holding forth about the best accommodations or the best comfort that could be found in new family arrangements, they would do well to ask themselves whether this was not a portent of the extinction of life and human presence on earth. Nowadays the only people who want to live as a family are ... homosexuals! They are demanding marriage, and some of them to have children, while the so-called 'normal people' have only one idea: to liquidate the family, to get rid of it." (Charles Melman, *L'homme sans gravité: Jouir à tout prix*. Interviews with Jean-Pierre Lebrun, January–August 2001–2002 [Paris: Denoël, 1st ed., 2003]).

11. Michel Schneider, "Lexique du ressentiment," *Le Débat*, no. 204 (2019). The argument about an "overly feminized" state and the critique of the "systematic" and "incestuous" drift of politics towards "feminine values" (generosity, sensitivity, gentleness) are defended, for example, in Michel Schneider, *Big Mother* (Paris: Odile Jacob, 2002).

12. Attacks are back in full swing. If we are to believe Jacques-Alain Miller, for example, the recent campaign against gender discrimination (where we see people hugging and reconciling, overcoming their differences in sexual

orientation) would "trample all decency underfoot." According to him, it "allows itself to enter the individual's most intimate realm," to "dictate behavior towards the father and mother, to the young and the old." It is no more nor less than an "abjection" aimed, in reality, at "censoring conduct" and "tampering with desire within the family" in order to "re-educate it." Jacques-Alain Miller, "L'École de la Tolérance," *Lacan Quotidien*, no. 930 (June 2, 2021): 5 (https://lacanquotidien.fr/blog/wp-content/uploads/2021/06/LQ-930.pdf).

13. Eighty psychoanalysts cry out: "Decolonial thought reinforces the narcissism of small differences," *Le Monde*, September 25, 2020. The following month's terrorist violence would serve as pretext for reinforcing this perspective, worthy of a Lépine competition for ideas of the extreme right. Intellectuals are going to call on the minister of education to intervene to control these dangerous thinkers at the university! "On Islamism, the Threat Is Denial," *Le Monde*, October 31, 2020.

14. Guy Hocquenghem, *Lettre ouverte à ceux qui sont passés du col Mao au Rotary* (Marseille: Agone, [1986] 2003). We cannot go into the clinical effects of reactionary prejudices *in practice* here. However, as you would expect, they are not without consequence. In my previous book, I dealt with this very question in relation to a certain conception of psychosis and the very particular political segregation to which people suffering from severe mental distress may be subjected, particularly in the context of patient presentations by certain Lacanian doctors. Florent Gabarron-Garcia, *L'héritage politique de la psychanalyse* [The Political Heritage of Psychoanalysis] (Paris: La Lenteur, 2018).

15. "Why this demand for equality? Why can't we stand difference? [...] It is curious that no one, I think, has pointed out that equality, which appears to us like an eminently

humanist and progressive watchword, is a death wish." Melman, *La nouvelle économie psychique*. Melman is speaking here specifically of equality between men and women.

16. Fortunately, there is now counterfire. We could cite, for example, the following books by psychoanalysts: Fabrice Bourlez, *Queer psychoanalyse, Clinique mineure et deconstructions du genre* [Queer Psychoanalysis: Minor Clinic and Gender Deconstructions] (Paris: Hermann, 2018); Karima Lazali, *Le trauma colonial, une enquête sur les effets psychiques et politiques contemporains de l'oppression colonial en Algérie* [Colonial Trauma: An Investigation into the Contemporary Psychic and Political Effects of Colonial Oppression in Algeria] (Paris, La Découverte, 2018); Thamy Ayouch, *Psychanalyse et hybridité, Genre, colonialité, subjectivations* [Psychoanalysis and Hybridity: Gender, Coloniality, Subjectification] (Leuven: Leuven University Press, 2018); Livio Boni and Sophie Mendelsohn, *La vie psychique du racism* [The Psychic Life of Racism] (Paris: La Découverte, 2021), and also my previous book, *L'héritage politique de la psychanalyse*. This book is a direct continuation of the previous one. We have freely reproduced some of its decisive elements concerning the perspective of a people's history. May the reader forgive me: this reworking was necessary in order to take this specific research further.

17. André Stéphane, *L'univers contestationnaire* [The Universe of Protest] (Paris: Payot, 1969).

18. Gilles Deleuze and Félix Guattari, *Anti-Oedipus: Capitalism and Schizophrenia*, trans. Robert Hurley, Mark Seem, and Helen R. Lane (Minneapolis: University of Minnesota Press, [1972] 1983).

19. I specifically analyzed the fate of Deleuze and Guattari's *Anti-Oedipus* in my previous book (Gabarron-Garcia, *L'héritage*). This book takes up some of its critical elements to explore in greater depth aspects that I had to postpone.

20. Alain Mijolla and Sophie Mijolla-Mellor, *Psychanalyse* (Paris: PUF, 1996), 792.
21. Jacques Hochmann's statement at the Utopsy seminar.
22. It would be a matter of contrasting "the pure gold of psychoanalysis" with the "lead of psychotherapy." But this is a translation error by Bernam in Freud's text, which inverts the meaning. Freud did not contrast "the gold of psychoanalysis" with the "lead of psychotherapy," but "gold" to "copper." Combined with gold, it is made even stronger (the "red gold" that jewelers use). Psychoanalism also seems not to note Freud's irony. "The gold of psychoanalysis" points to a fantasy of purity that Freud could already detect in some of his colleagues.
23. Jacques-Alain Miller, "Lacan et la politique," *Cités*, no. 16 (2003): 105–23.
24. François Furet, *Penser la Révolution française* [Thinking the French Revolution] (Paris: Galimard, 1978).
25. Jacques André, *La révolution fratricide* [Fratricidal Revolution] (Paris: PUF, 1993). From the "murder of the father" with Louis XVI's execution to the short period of 1789–91 of fraternity, an expression of the "actors' latent homosexuality" that "does not yet reveal the ravages of its ambivalence," to the "failure of the Constitution" that leads to the Terror, because it "calls into question the principle of representation, of mediation, by a paternal authority." From that point on, it is all over: the king can be killed but his principle must be enshrined in the Constitution. Without a paternal third, the revolution "turns against itself," the Terror where "brothers kill each other." The idea of a possible non-representative direct democracy seems unthinkable for the author.
26. Paul-Laurent Assoun, *Tuer le mort, le désir révolutionnaire* [Killing Death: Revolutionary Desire] (Paris: PUF, 2015).

27. Jacques-Alain Miller, "Communiqué pour Rafah Nached," *La règle du jeu*, September 13, 2011 (https://laregledujeu.org/2011/09/13/7095/jacques-alainmiller-sengage-pour-la-liberation-derafah-nached/).
28. I also share his views. Robert Castel, *Le psychanalysme, l'ordre psychanalytique et le pouvoir* [Psychoanalism, Psychoanalytic Order and Power] (Paris: Maspero, 1973).
29. Aurel Kolnai, *Psychoanalyse und Soziologie* (Vienna: Internationaler Psychoanalytischer Verlag, 1920).

1. Freud Looks East: Vera Schmidt and Psychoanalysis in the Land of the Soviets

1. Sigmund Freud, *Civilization and Its Discontents* (1930). Obviously, cultural pessimism appears earlier in his work, but on a much smaller scale.
2. Without presenting the qualities of Hobbes's thought, psychoanalism fails here in a demonological metaphysics: "It's human nature to enjoy what is dirty, or, if you prefer, improper, impure, and to never give up the desire to be evil" (Schneider, *Big Mother*, 11). It's thus easy to understand the naturally authoritarian (and paternalist) politics that is needed to avoid the war of all against all.
3. Jones's perspective is still an authority in these analytic circles, even though it has been widely challenged by most historians.
4. Ernest Jones, *The Life and Work of Sigmund Freud*, vol. 3 (New York: Basic Books, 1953), 343.
5. Paul-Laurent Assoun, "Freudisme et indifférentisme politique" [Freud and Political Indifferentism], *Hermès*, nos. 5–6 (1989): 346.

6. Sigmund Freud, *The Future of an Illusion*, trans. James Strachey (New York: W.W. Norton & Company, [1927] 1961), 12.
7. Ibid. 10.
8. Freud's previous texts, where the concepts from *Civilization and Its Discontents* are linked to a political critique, suffer the same fate. However, this political critique can be found in several texts, for example in "'Civilized' Sexual Morality and Modern Nervous Illness."
9. Freud, *The Future of an Illusion*, 39.
10. Ibid., 43.
11. Acknowledging the "purely human origin of all the regulations and precepts of civilization [...] along with their pretended sanctity, these commandments and laws would lose their rigidity and unchangeableness as well. People could understand that they are made, not so much to rule them as, on the contrary, to serve their interests; and they would adopt a more friendly attitude to them" and "would aim only at their improvement." Freud, *The Future of an Illusion*, 47.
12. The fundamental prohibitions: murder, incest, cannibalism.
13. Freud, *The Future of an Illusion*, 12.
14. Ibid., 46.
15. Jean Marti, "La Psychanalyse en Russie: 1909–1930," *Critique*, no. 346 (1976); Martin Miller, *Freud and the Bolsheviks: Psychoanalysis in Imperial Russia and the Soviet Union* (New Haven: Yale University Press, 1998). Of course, Freud had reservations about the idea that religion had to be suppressed "by force and at a single blow." But to take up one of Marx's arguments that religion is the opium of the people, and to turn his criticism towards the situation in the United States:

the believer will not let his belief be torn from him, either by arguments or by prohibitions [...] A man who has been taking sleeping draughts for tens of years is naturally unable to sleep if his sleeping draught is taken away from him. That the effect of religious consolations may be likened to that of a narcotic is well illustrated by what is happening in America. There they are now trying ... , intoxicants, and other pleasure-producing substances, and instead, by way of compensation, are surfeiting them with piety. (Freud, *The Future of an Illusion*, 49)

16. Wilhelm Reich, *The Function of the Orgasm*, trans. Vincent R. Carfagno (New York: Farrar, Straus, and Giroux, 1973), 211.
17. Freud, *The Future of an Illusion*, 8–9.
18. Ibid., 9.
19. Ibid., 48–50.
20. Marti, "La psychanalyse en Russie," 235.
21. Sigmund Freud and Sándor Ferenczi, *Correspondance*, vol. 2, *1914–1919* (Paris: Calmann-Lévy, 1996), 331.
22. Elizabeth Ann Danto, *Freud's Free Clinics: Psychoanalysis and Social Justice, 1918–1938* (New York: Columbia University Press, 2005). For this chapter, I have freely reproduced analyses from this historian and the two articles translated in French in the journal *Le Coq-Héron* (her book has still not been translated into French), as well as analyses from Russell Jacoby's book *The Repression of Psychoanalysis*.
23. At the other end of the revisionist spectrum, there are also the anticommunist historians who claim that Freud's policinics were financed by the KGB through Eitingon (Alexander Etkind, *Eros of the Impossible: The History of Psychoanalysis in Russia* [Westview Press, 1996]).

24. Sigmund Freud, "Lines of Advance in Psycho-Analytic Therapy."
25. It is astonishing to see how a certain orthodoxy of psychoanalism retains only those of Freud's texts that treat the "inconveniences" of free access (notably his 1913 article, "On Beginning the Treatment") and "forgets" the official moment of promoting free treatment.
26. Cited by Elizabeth Ann Danto, "Une révolution dans 'l'âme de l'homme,'" *Le Coq-Héron*, no. 201 (2010): 28.
27. Jean-Michel Palmier, "La psychanalyse en Hongrie," in Roland Jaccard, ed., *Histoire de la psychanalyse*, vol. 2 (Paris, Hachette, 1982), 165; Michelle Moreau-Ricaud, "La psychanalyse à l'université: histoire de la première chaire, Budapest avril 1919–juillet 1919," *Psychanalyse à l'université*, vol. 15, no. 60 (1990); Arpad Kadarkay, *Georg Lukács: Life, Thought and Politics* (Oxford: Basil Blackwell, 1991).
28. Freud and Ferenczi, *Correspondance*, vol. 2, 1914–1919, 342.
29. Leon Trotsky, "Austrian Social Democracy: Victor Adler," *Political Profiles*, July 1913 www.marxists.org/archive/trotsky/profiles/victoradler.htm.
30. Mireille Cifali and Jeanne Moll, *Pédagogie et psychanalyse* (Paris: Dunod, 1985).
31. Hans-Joachim Rothe, *Karl Landauer: Theorie der Affekte und andere Schriften zur Ich-Organisation* (Frankfurt: Fischer Taschenbuch, 1991).
32. Constantin Sinelnikoff, "La vie militante de Wilhelm Reich," in *L'oeuvre de Wilhelm Reich*, vol. 1 (Paris: Maspero, 1970), 15.
33. Danto, *Freud's Free Clinics*.
34. Danto, "Une revolution."
35. Cited by Danto, *Freud's Free Clinics*.
36. Danto, *Freud's Free Clinics*, 7.
37. Freud, "Lines of Advance," 3635.

38. Gilles Tréhel, "Ernst Simmel (1882–1947): Psychanalyse des masses," *L'information psychiatrique* (2016): 327–335.
39. Freud and Fereczi, *Correspondance*, vol. 2, 1914–1919, 384.
40. Miller, *Freud and the Bolsheviks*, 66.
41. Wilhelm Reich, *Reich parle de Freud* (Paris: Payot, 1972), 33.
42. Clara Zetkin, "Lenin on the Women's Question," in *The Emancipation of Women: From the Writings of V. I. Lenin* (International Publishers, 1966), 101.
43. Made up of some of the poorest peasants, these communes were initially supported by Bolshevik power. They represent "the most successful attempt of realizing the communist and libertarian ideal: direct democracy, radical equality, and human fellowship." See Éric Aunoble, *Le communism, tout de suite: Le movement des communes dans l'Ukraine soviétique* [Communism Now: The Commune Movement in Soviet Ukraine] (Paris: Les Nuits Rouges, 2008). As Aunoble points out, *kommunard* and *communist* were then considered synonyms.
44. Alexandra Kollontaï, *Sexual Relations and the Class Struggle: Love and the New Morality* (Bristol: Falling Wall Press, 1972). According to Alexander Goikhbarg, the young author of the new Family Code, the aim was to prepare the ground for a "time" when the "fetters between husband and wife" would become "obsolete." Commenting on the "spirit of the laws" introduced then, he argues, "'Proletarian power constructs its codes and all of its laws dialectically, so that every day of their existence undermines the need for their existence.' In short, the aim of law was 'to make law superfluous'" (A. G. Goikhbarg, "Pervyi kodeks Zakonov RSFSR", *Proletarskaia revoliutsiia i pravo*, no. 7 (1918), cited by Wendy Goldman, *Women, the State and the Revolution: Soviet Family Policy and Social Life*,

1917–1936 (Cambridge: Cambridge University Press, 1993), 1.

45. I translate "ce courant libertaire" as "liberatory current," since "libertarian" has taken on a right reactionary meaning in (US) English. In the European context, libertarian tends to be another name for anarchism, which is so often written out of history. [Translator's note.]

46. For more on these issues, see, among others, Arthur Clech, "Révolutions russes: l'émergence et l'affirmation d'une conscience de soi homosexuelle ?" [Russian Revolutions: The Emergence and Affirmation of a Homosexual Self-Conscioussness], *Comment s'en sortir*, no. 5, *Le sexe de la révolution* (2017).

47. Trotsky took his wife's name, Sedova.

48. Goldman, *Women, the State, and the Revolution*.

49. Florence Tamagne, "The World League for Sexual Reform: A Homosexual Internationale?" in *A History of Homosexuality in Europe: Berlin, London, Paris 1919–1939*, 2 vols. (New York: Algora Publishing, 2006).

50. Richard Stites, *Revolutionary Dreams: Utopian Vision and Experimental Life in the Russian Revolution* (Oxford: Oxford University Press, 1989).

51. As Anna Maria Accerboni writes, "Freud knew her and considered her training sufficiently serious to recognize her as a psychoanalyst." Along with Sabina Spielrein, she was one of the four Russian members of the Vienna Psychoanalytic Society. Anna Maria Accerboni, "Tatiana Rosenthal, une brève saison analytique" [Tatiana Rosenthal, A Brief Season of Analysis] *Revue internationale d'histoire de la psychanalyse* [International Review of the History of Psychoanalysis] (1992): 97.

52. Marti, "La psychanalyse en Russie," 205.

53. Miller, *Freud and the Bolsheviks*, 56.

54. However, it is worth noting that one exception is Jones, who was reluctant to see these Russian psychoanalysts join the IPA, necessitating the intervention of Abraham and Freud. Marti, "La psychanalyse en Russie," 215–16.
55. Melanie Klein, *Contributions to Psychoanalysis, 1921–1945* (London: Hogarth Press, 1948), 67.
56. She thus accomplished Tatiana Rosenthal's idea. See Accerboni, "Tatiana Rosenthal," 102.
57. Sándor Ferenczi, "Psycho-analysis and Pedagogy," *International Journal of Psychoanalysis*, vol. 39 (1908): 220.
58. Cited by F. V. Garmonov, " La planification de l'enseignement en URSS" [The Planning of Teaching in the USSR], *Revue du tiers-monde* (1960): 85.
59. Sigmund Freud, "The Sexual Enlightenment of Children (An Open Letter to Dr. M. Fürst)," in *The Complete Psychological Works of Sigmund Freud* ([1907] 1918). On the fear of thinking instilled in women by education and religion, see also the text "'Civilized' Sexual Morality and Modern Nervous Illness" (1908).
60. Here we take up part of Jean-Marie Brohm's analysis, "Presentation," in Vera Schmidt and Annie Reich, eds., *Pulsions sexuelles et éducation du corps* [Sexual Drives and Education of the Body] (Paris, 10/18, 1979), 15–29.
61. Melanie Klein, *Contributions to Psycho-analysis*, 32.
62. Vera Schmidt, "Éducation psychanalytique en Russie soviétique" [Psychoanalytic Education in Soviet Russia], in Vera Schmidt and Annie Reich, eds., *Pulsions sexuelles et éducation du corps* (Paris, 10/18, 1979), 66.
63. Ibid., 65.
64. Ibid., 64.
65. Ibid., 66.
66. Freud, *The Future of an Illusion*, 47.
67. Ibid.
68. Freud, "The Sexual Enlightenment of Children."

69. Ibid.
70. Freud, *The Future of an Illusion*, 48.

2. Wilhelm Reich: From the Vienna Policlinic to the Sexpol in Berlin

1. He finished his studies in 1922 and 1924 respectively.
2. Wilhelm Reich, *The Function of the Orgasm*, 29.
3. Ibid., 40–41.
4. Ibid., 48.
5. Ibid.
6. Ibid., 144.
7. Wilhelm Reich, *Reich Speaks of Freud* (New York: Farrar, Strauss and Giroux, 1967), 152.
8. Richard Sterba, *Reminiscences of a Viennese Psychoanalyst* (Detroit: Wayne State University Press, 1982), 34–5.
9. Before setting up his seminar, he held meetings of young analysts more of less officially. These were already frowned upon by the "elders." Richard Sterba says that his own analyst, Hitschmann, "forbade [him] to attend the private meetings of the younger members," which gave him "the impression that some of the older members were jealous of the eagerness of the younger members to further their analytic growth and knowledge." Sterba, *Reminiscences*, 30.
10. Freud still supported Reich in 1930 in his correspondence with Federn (cf. *Cartes postales, notes, lettres de Sigmund Freud à Paul Federn, 1905–1938* [Post Cards, Notes, Letters from Sigmund Freud to Paul Federn, 1905–1938] [Paris: Ithaque, 2018]). It is also worth noting that Paul Federn was Wilhelm Reich's analyst and probably showed a massive, unanalyzed negative countertransference towards his young patient (at that time, this problem

had not yet been clearly formulated). On these questions (and on the hostility of some of his Viennese colleagues), see Lore Reich Rubin, "Wilhelm Reich and Anna Freud: His Expulsion from Psychoanalysis," *International Forum of Psychoanalysis*, vol. 12 (2003). Finally, we should mention that Federn is the author of an essay in which he analyzes the postwar generation's challenge to authority as an unconscious parricide aiming to establish a "society without a father" (*Zur Psychologie der Revolution: Die vaterlose Gesellschaft* [On the Psychology of Revolution: The Fatherless Society] [Leipzig: Suschitzky, 1919]). We can assume that Reich's arrival in Vienna and the importance he took on in the analytic movement confirmed this dubious thesis in his view.

11. Current neurosis includes anxiety neurosis and neurasthenia.
12. Just like his early articles: "Coition and the Sexes" (1921) and "Concerning Specific Forms of Masturbation" (1922), in Wilhelm Reich, *Early Writings*, vol. 1, trans. Philip Schmitz (New York: Farrar, Straus, and Giroux: 1975).
13. Freud cites abstinence, coitus interruptus, or excessive masturbation. "Sexuality in the Aetiology of the Neurosis" (1898).
14. For a detailed account of Reich's concepts and his dialogue with analytic theories, please refer to Constantin Sinelnikoff, *L'Oeuvre de Wilhelm Reich* [The Work of Wilhelm Reich] (Paris: Les Nuits Rouges, 2nd ed., [1970] 2002), 53–75. In general, we endorse many of his brilliant analyses in this chapter on Reich. We also rely—to a lesser extent—on Jean-Michel Palmier's book, *Wilhelm Reich* (Paris: 10/18, 1969).
15. Having strayed from its original objective of serving the most disadvantaged, the Berlin Institute developed an authoritarian hierarchical structure that the youngest

analysts denounced and that prevented any political discussion.

16. Reich, *Function of the Orgasm*, 74.
17. Ibid., 76.
18. Ibid., 80.
19. Wilhelm Reich, *The Impulsive Character*, trans. Barbara G. Koopman (New York: Meridian, 1974), 37, cited by Sinelnikoff, *L'Oeuvre de Wilhelm Reich*, 73. For a detailed study of the issues at stake in this work, please refer to Sinelnikoff's book.
20. Reich, *The Function of the Orgasm*, 75. This is still largely the case.
21. Ibid., 76. This had already been suggested by Aichhorn in a series of lectures published in 1925 with the title *Verwahrloste Jugend* [Neglected Youth] (Vienna: Internationaler Psychoanalytischer Verlag, 1925)
22. Reich, *The Function of the Orgasm*, 76–7.
23. Ibid., 77.
24. Ibid., 77–8.
25. Ibid., 76.
26. Ibid., 78.
27. Ibid., 75.
28. This foray into contemporary ethnology would come into contradiction with Freud's views on the matter. Freud drew on the older evolutionist theories of Lamarck and Darwin, from whom he derived his concept of culture coming from the "primitive horde," incest, and the Oedipus complex. Freud's universalist and naturalizing anthropology would be discussed and challenged by social and cultural anthropology, notably Malinowski, who demonstrated how the matrilineal societies of the Trobriand Islands escaped the supposed universalism of Oedipus. Malinowski's approach inspired Reich's research into anthropology.

29. Wilhelm Reich, *People in Trouble*, trans. Philip Schmitz (New York: Farrar, Straus, and Giroux), 73.
30. Reich, *The Function of the Orgasm*, 195.
31. Ibid., 191.
32. Reich, *People in Trouble*, 105.
33. Ibid., 106.
34. Four psychoanalysts, three obstetricians, and a lawyer participated.
35. Reich, *People in Trouble*, 113.
36. Freud, "'Civilized' Sexual Morality and Modern Nervous Illness" (1908).
37. Freud, *The Future of an Illusion*, 48.
38. Reich, *People in Trouble*, 110–11.
39. Ibid., 110.
40. Ibid., 111–12.
41. Ibid., 114.
42. Reich, *The Function of the Orgasm*, 128.
43. Sigmund Freud, *Beyond the Pleasure Principle*.
44. Theodor Reik, *The Compulsion to Confess: On the Psychoanalysis of Crime and Punishment* (New York: Grove Press, [1925] 1961).
45. Otto Fenichel, "Psychoanalyse der Politik : Eine Kritik" [Psychoanalysis of Politics: A Critique], *Psychoanalytische Bewegung*, vol. 4 (1932): 256–9.
46. Wilhelm Reich, *The Invasion of Compulsory Sex-Morality*, trans. Werner Grossmann and Doreen Grossmann (New York: Farrar, Straus, and Giroux, 1971), xxvi.
47. He was also the first president of Interpol.
48. Sinelnikoff, *L'Oeuvre de Wilhelm Reich*, 164.
49. Sterba, *Reminiscences*, 111.
50. As proof of this, Bernfeld, a politically engaged analyst, wrote a text in 1929 that made this issue clear.
51. In a letter dated October 10, 1930, Freud writes: "Dear Doctor, in our discussions we have come to the conclu-

sion that your temporary move to Berlin should not entail the loss of your positions in Vienna, I think it is important to point this out." Letter from Freud to Reich, cited by Karl Fallen, *Willhelm Reich, Psychoanalyse und Politik* (Salzburg: Geyer, 1988), 201. This was not the position of Anna Freud, who finally forced Reich to choose between Vienna and Berlin, arguing that he could not be a psychoanalyst member in Vienna and Berlin at the same time. At this time, Anna Freud already wanted to drive Reich out. This was the first step in his future exclusion. Reich abandoned his position in Vienna. There will be more on this later.

52. Reich, *People in Trouble*, 143.
53. Here we freely adopt Sinelnikoff's analyses, *L'Oeuvre de Wilhelm Reich*, 31–8.
54. Reich, *People in Trouble*, 149.
55. Wilhelm Reich, *What Is Class Consciousness?* (London: Socialist Reproduction, 1971).
56. Reich, *What Is Class Consciousness?*
57. The league's aims were primarily practical: It was a matter of reforming sex. The league was inspired by the Bolsheviks' first sexual reforms. Though it was officially apolitical, many of its members were communists. The platform proposed by Reich was therefore very well received by these members. See Atina Grossmann, *Reforming Sex: The German Movement for Birth Control and Abortion Reform 1920–1950* (Oxford: Oxford University Press, 1995).
58. Wilhelm Reich, *The Mass Psychology of Fascism*, trans. Vincent R. Carfagno (New York: Farrar, Straus, and Giroux, 1970), 21.
59. Ibid., 68.
60. Reich, *What Is Class Consciousness?*, 2.
61. Reich, *People in Trouble*, 140–1.
62. Reich, *What Is Class Consciousness?*, 8.
63. Reich, *People in Trouble*, 234.

3. The Future of Freudian Pessimism

1. Let's add that this, however, does not make Freud a communist.
2. Freud, *The Future of an Illusion*, 53.
3. This is an old theme in the analytic field, dating back to the 1910s, with James Putnam, the founder of the American Society of Neurology.
4. It's true that the dogma doesn't usually bother with this kind of questioning. It therefore commits a triple error. Exegetically, it does not do justice to the evolution of Freud's work. Historically, it says nothing about the progressive psychoanalytic practices Freud promoted in the 1920s, nor about the practices which, in contrast, would be defended by his association in the name of so-called psychoanalytic neutrality after 1929 and Hitler's rise to power. Finally, ideologically, this reading fetishizes a late moment in Freud's articulations by isolating it from its context and from the debates and the sometimes contradictory practices then prevailing in the analytic world.
5. To be more precise, we are thinking here of the Trotskyite left: the libertarian branch that was crushed early on.
6. Richard Stites, *The Women's Liberation Movement in Russia: Feminism, Nihilism, and Bolshevism, 1860–1930* (Princeton: Princeton University Press, 1978).
7. For example, we find this very fragmented contextualization (as if "in reverse") in Jean-Michel Quinodoz, *Lire Freud* [Reading Freud] (Paris: PUF, 2004), 263. "A pessimistic or a realistic view of the human condition?": between Scylla and Charybdis, this is the typical reading program of *Civilization and Its Discontents* generally recommended for students in order to "read Freud properly."

8. Freud, *The Future of an Illusion*, 48–9. He repeats this statement a little further on: "If experience should show ... that we have been mistaken, we will give up our expectations" (53).
9. He had been suffering from cancer for several years and underwent thirty-one highly painful operations, most of which involved removing leukoplakia associated with malignant tumors.
10. Freud, *Civilization and Its Discontents*.
11. Of course, this pessimism had been expressed long before in Freud's work (for example, see: "On the Universal Tendency to Debasement in the Sphere of Love"). But as in the case of the *Weltanschauung* issue and debate, we are witnessing a kind of "flare up" here.
12. We have already mentioned how psychoanalism missed the political stakes of *The Future of an Illusion*, but it is also worth mentioning that it says nothing of the elements of theoretical continuity that remain in *Civilization* despite everything. According to psychoanalism, Freud's pessimism must be total, unmitigated, and eternal. But if it is true that Freud asserts in *Civilization* that there are "difficulties attaching to the nature of civilization which will not yield to any attempt at reform," psychoanalism doesn't emphasize the fact that, *at the same time*, Freud always *maintains* the necessity and possibility of reforms in this book:

> When we justly find fault with the present state of our civilization for so inadequately fulfilling our demands for a plan of life that shall make us happy, and for allowing the existence of so much suffering which could probably be avoided—when, with unsparing criticism, we try to uncover the roots of its imperfection, we are undoubtedly exercising a proper right and are not showing ourselves enemies of civilization. We may expect gradually to carry

though such alterations in our civilization as will better satisfy our needs and will escape our criticisms.

Finally, in *Civilization* Freud also maintains his political critique of the excessive sexual repression very specific to "Western culture":

> In this respect civilization behaves towards sexuality as a people or a stratum of its population does which has subjected another one to its exploitation. Fear of a revolt by the suppressed elements drives it to stricter precautionary measures. A high-water mark in such a development has been reached in our Western European civilization.

And society "cannot in any way be justified in going to the length of actually *disavowing* such easily demonstrable, and, indeed, striking phenomena." Although it is seriously understated, Freud by no means excludes the necessity and the relevance of intervention towards social justice. In short, psychoanalism goes astray when it insists on Thanatos to the point of giving the impression that it is the *unilateral* metapsychological truth about the unconscious that psychoanalysis reveals. Eros is never far away. Moreover, Freud ends *Civilization* by invoking its principle: "And now it is to be expected that the other of the two 'Heavenly Powers,' eternal Eros, will make an effort to assert himself in the struggle with his equally immortal adversary." Freud makes it clear that no one can "foresee" the success or result.

13. A highly developed three volumes, Ernest Jones, *The Life and Work of Sigmund Freud* (New York: Basic Books, 1957).
14. Bernd Nitzschke, "Psychoanalysis as a Non-political Science," *Zeitschrift für Psychosomatische Medizin und Psychoanalyse*, vol. 37, no. 1 (February 1991): 31–44.

15. Sigmund Freud, "The Question of a *Weltanshcauung*," Lecture XXXV in *New Introductory Lectures on Psycho-Analysis* (1933). This text is also known under the more "classic" title—due to an older translation: "A Concept of the Universe."
16. Max Eitingon, "Lettre 754 E," in Sigmund Freud and Max Eitingon, *Correspondance 1906–1939*, ed. Michael Schöter (Paris: Hachette Littératures), 784.
17. Sigmund Freud, "Letter 755 F," in Sigmund Freud and Max Eitingon, *Correspondance 1906–1939*, 785.
18. Max Eitingon, "Letter 756 E," March 24 1933, in Sigmund Freud and Max Eitingon, *Correspondance 1906–1939*, 786.
19. Karen Brecht, Volker Friedrich, Ludger M. Hermanns, Isidor J. Kaminer, and Dirk Juelich, *Ici la vie continue d'une manière fort surprenante* [Here Life Goes On in a Most Surprising Way] (Paris: Association Internationale d'Histoire de la Psychanalyse, 1985), 150–7.
20. Freud, "Letter 759 F," in Sigmund Freud and Max Eitingon, *Correspondance 1906–1939*, 789.
21. "He agreed to expel Reich," Freud, "Letter 759 F3," in Sigmund Freud and Max Eitingon, *Correspondance 1906–1939*, 789. For his part, Boehm testifies to Freud's explicit wish to "free him from Reich." Felix Boehm cited by Nitzschke, "Psychoanalysis as Non-political Science." Regarding all of these questions, please refer to the book Nitzschke wrote with Fallend, *Der "Fall" Wilhelm Reich, Beiträge zum Verhältnis von Psychoanalyse und Politik* [The "Case" of Wilhelm Reich: Contributions to the Relationship between Psychoanalysis and Politics] (Frankfurt am Maim: Suhrkamp Taschenbuch, 1997, reprinted 2002).
22. According to Reich's daughter, Anna Freud also worked alongside Jones to influence Freud to expel Reich. Lore Reich Rubin, "Wilhelm Reich and Anna Freud: His

Expulsion from Psychoanalysis," *International Forum of Psychoanalysis*, vol. 12, nos. 2–3 (2003): 109–17.
23. Freud, "The Question of a *Weltanschauung*."
24. Freud, *New Introductory Lectures on Psycho-Analysis*.
25. Reich was in fact on the lists drawn up by the Gestapo.
26. This was secret and could not be made official, since Reich's influence was considerable in the analytic world at the time.
27. "We should not kick Reich out, especially now." Max Eitingon, "Letter 760 E," April 21, 1933, in Sigmund Freud and Max Eitingon, *Correspondance 1906–1939*, 792.
28. Geoffrey Cocks, *Psychotherapy in the Third Reich: The Göring Institute* (Oxford: Oxford University Press, 1987), 90.
29. This letter from Reich in 1933 can be found in the secret circulars that Fenichel established in 1934.
30. Cited by Nitzschke, "Psychoanalysis as a Nonpolitical Science," 174. Here we take up part of Nitzschke's reading.
31. Reich's latest insights into political psychoanalysis were welcomed and supported by many analysts, even in the 1930s. For example, there are reports from Otto Fenichel, Erich Fromm (1932), Karl Laudauer (1934), and Max Horkheimer (1936).
32. During his exile, he joined the Norwegian Psychoanalytic Society, whose application to the IPA was rejected: Reich could never become a member of the association again. Lore Reich Rubin, "Wilhelm Reich and Anna Freud."
33. Apart from Fenichel, who raised some formal objections, the analysts close to Reich (or his ideas) all kept quiet. This silence on such violence accentuates the effectiveness of its perversity, as well as its mark on the analytic institution—which seemed to persist in many psychoanalytic schools that remained in denial about the political question.

34. It consists of more than 2,500 typed pages of exceptional documentation of the analytic movement that have yet to be translated into French.
35. Otto Fenichel, *Rundbrief* 1, March 1934, box 1, folder 1, Austen Riggs Library.
36. Jones's letter to Anna Freud (*Ici la vie continue*, 114–15) and Boehm's account (*Ici la vie continue*, 116–17).
37. Gilles Perrault, *The Red Orchestra*, trans. Peter Wiles (New York: Simon and Schuster, 1969). Among other things, Rittmeister wrote a "prison diary" in which the coherence of his engaged career—both political and psychoanalytic—is, according to Sigg's indications, comparable to that of Marie Langer, to whom we'll return later. Bernard W. Sigg, "Psychanalystes debout," *Revue internationale d'histoire de la psychanalyse* (Paris: PUF, 1992), 320–1.
38. Régine Lockot, "À propos des changements de noms de l'association psychanalytique de Berlin," *La revue lacanienne*, vol. 1 (2008): 28.
39. Nitzschke, "Psychoanalysis as Nonpolitical Science." During a meeting in Basel, Jones describes his encounter with Matthias Göring, who seemed "fairly amiable and amenable." In a cryptic style that removes the tragedy of history and his personal compromise of principles, Jones adds: "but it turned out later that he was not in a position to fulfil the promises he made me about the degree of freedom that was to be allowed the psycho-analytical group." Jones, *Life and Work of Sigmund Freud*, 620. However, as early as May 1936, before the Marienbad Congress, Göring, in his inaugural speech at the new German Institute (in which Jones is quoted alongside Hitler), made it abundantly clear: There could be no psychotherapy without a National Socialist *Weltanschauung*.
40. Lockot, "À propos des changements de noms...," 28.

41. Cited in Jacoby, *Repression*, 100. In hindsight, Fenichel realized that Edith Jacobson and he had made a mistake and that Reich had been right: It would have been better purely and simply to dissolve the German Society in the summer of 1933.
42. Sterba, *Reminiscences*, 164–5.
43. Ibid., 163.
44. Ernest Jones, "Opening Speech," *International Journal of Psychoanalysis, Bulletin of the International Psycho-Analytical Association*, vol. 30 (1949): 178–208.
45. Of course, the Frankfurt School experienced a decisive postwar revival, but under the auspices of critical theory and philosophy (with Adorno, Marcuse, etc.) rather than a revolutionary analytic practice. Indeed, Mitscherlich, their representative psychoanalyst, who founded the Sigmund Freud Institute in 1960, defended an analytic practice within the political coordinates of liberalism ... for which Marcuse violently criticized him. Gérard Raulet, *La philosophie allemande depuis 1945* [German Philosophy after 1945] (Paris: Armand Colin, 2006).
46. Nicolas Gougoulis, "Les centres de consultation psychanalytiques dans leur histoires" [The History of Psychoanalytic Consultation Centers], *Le Coq-Héron* (2010): 50.

4. Marie Langer: From 1930s Vienna to 1970s Latin America

1. Marie Langer, *Mémoria, historia y dialoguo psicanalitico* [Memory, History, and Psychoanalytic Dialogue] (Buenos Aires: Folios Ediciones, 1984), 52 [French trans. by the author].
2. M. Langer, *Mémoria, historia y dialoguo psicanalitico*, 3.
3. Ibid., 14, 4.

4. Among other examples of this liberation, Marie Langer mentions that women no longer had to wear corsets, and that her parents were going to dance the Charleston, as well as Magnus Hirschfeld claiming homosexuals as the "third sex."
5. M. Langer, *Mémoria, historia y dialoguo psicanalitico*, 14.
6. Ibid., 20.
7. Ibid., 9.
8. Ibid., 206.
9. Marie Langer, " Psicoanalisis y/o révolucion social" [Psychoanalysis and/or Social Revoution], in *Cuestionamos* [Questioning] (Buenos Aires: Granica Editor, 1971), 260.
10. M. Langer, *Mémoria, historia y dialoguo psicanalitico*, 55.
11. M. Langer, " Psicoanalisis y/o révolucion social," 260.
12. Marie Langer, "El analizando del 2000" [Analyzing the 2000s], *Revue Argentina de Psicoanalítico*, vol. 25 (2000): 629.
13. Contrary to what Geneviève Morel says, these aren't "Langer's contradictions" but rather those of the analytic institution and its alleged neutrality. Geneviève Morel, "Les contradictions d'une psychanalyste au xxe siècle" [A Psychoanalyst's Contradictions in the Twentieth Century], in Susana Elkin and Martin Reca, eds., *Marie Langer: Une psychanalyste féministe en Argentine* [Marie Langer: A Feminist Psychoanalyst in Argentine] (Paris: L'Harmattan, 2017).
14. M. Langer, *Mémoria, historia y dialoguo psicanalitico*, 60.
15. Veronica Langer, "Marie Langer et le prince charmant" [Marie Langer and Prince Charming], in Elkin et Reca, *Une psychanalyste féministe en Argentine*, 33.
16. M. Langer, *Mémoria, historia y dialoguo psicanalitico*, 60.
17. Ibid., 62.
18. Ibid., 66.
19. Marie Langer, "Psicoanalisis y/o révolucion social," 79.
20. MLanger, *Mémoria, historia y dialoguo psicanalitico*, 81–2.

21. To illustrate the point, we could evoke certain contemporary French Lacanian schools.
22. M. Langer, *Mémoria, historia y dialoguo psicanalitico*, 82.
23. V. Langer, "Marie Langer et le prince charmant," 34.
24. M. Langer, *Mémoria, historia y dialoguo psicanalitico*, 87.
25. M. Langer, "La mujer, sus limitaciones, y potencialidades" [The Limitations and Potentialities of Women], *Cuestianomos*, vol. 1/2, 1987, 200.
26. Álvarez Del Castillo, *Izquierda freudiana, Plataforma internacional: cuarenta anos de historia y legado* [Freudian Left, International Platform: Forty Years of History and Legacy] (Mexico: Monterray, 2012), p. 141.
27. Ibid., 16.
28. Ginsberg, E. "Marx y Freud, delicuentos ideologicos" [Marx and Freud: Ideological Delinquents], *Cuardenos de marcha I* (Buenos Aires, 1977), 73–81.
29. M. Langer, " Psicoanalisis y/o révolucion social," 15.
30. The CDI aimed to train mental health workers in psychoanalysis and "the context of a class-divided society."
31. We should also mention the Documento movement led by Fernando Ulloa and concomitant with Plataforma Argentina, which shared, for the most part, its critical view of the APA, as well as its political orientation.
32. Collectif, "En este numero" [In This Issue], *Los libros* (1972): 2.
33. Del Castillo, *Izquierda freudiana*, 142.
34. As Lucia Bley rightly observes, "the exact word used is 'encastillar,' which literally means gather people in a castle ('castillo')." Lucia Bley, "Marie Langer ou l'impossible neutralité de la psychanalyse" [Marie Langer, or Psychoanalysis's Impossible Neutrality], *Topiques* (Paris: L'esprit du temps, 2017).
35. Del Castillo, *Izquierda freudiana*, 149.
36. Ibid., 50–1.

37. M. Langer, *Mémoria, historia y dialoguo psicanalitico*, 175.
38. Ibid., 194.
39. Ibid., 193–4.
40. M. Langer, "La mujer, sus limitaciones, y potencialidades," 151.
41. Helena Besserman Vianna, *Politique de la psychanalyse face à la dictature et à la torture: N'en parlez àpersonne* [The Politics of Psychoanalysis Facing Dictatorship and Torture: Don't Tell Anyone] (Paris, L'Harmattan, 1997).

5. From the Catalonian Commune to La Borde Clinic

1. François Tosquelles, "Une politique de la folie" [A Politics of Madness], *Chimères*, vol. 13 (Autumn 1991): 70. The text featured in *Chimères* is taken from the film, *Tosquelles, une politique de la folie*, directed with commentary by François Pain, Danièle Sivadon, and Jean-Claude Polack. It was released in 1990.
2. George Orwell, *Homage to Catalonia* (London: Alma Classics, [1938] 2022), 6–7.
3. François Tosquelles, "Une politique de la folie," 69.
4. François Tosquelles, "La guerre d'Espagne" [The Spanish War], *Vie social et traitements*, vol. 72 (1987): 135–6.
5. Ibid., 136.
6. Ibid., 137.
7. François Tosquelles, "Une politique de la folie," 71.
8. Ibid.
9. Carlos Semprún Maura, *Révolution et contre-révolution en Catalogne* [Revolution and Counter-revolution in Catalonia] (Paris: Éditions Mame, 1974); Pierre Broué and Émile Témine, *La Révolution et la guerre d'Espagne* [The Revolution and the Spanish War] (Paris: Minuit, 1996); Frédéric Goldbronn and Frank Mintz, "Quand l'Espagne révolu-

tionnaire vivait en anarchie" [When Revolutionary Spain Lived in Anarchy], *Le Monde diplomatique* (December 2000).
10. François Tosquelles, "Une politique de la folie," 72.
11. François Tosquelles, "La guerre d'Espagne," 136.
12. Ibid.
13. Ibid.
14. Quoted in Anne Mathieu, "En 1939, plongée dans les camps de réfugiés espagnols en France" [A Dive into the Spanish Refugee Camps in France in 1939], *Le Monde diplomatique* (August 2019).
15. Geneviève Dreyfus-Armand, *L'exil des républicains en France* [The Republicans' Exile in France] (Paris: Albin Michel, 1999).
16. François Tosquelles, "Une politique de la folie," 73.
17. Isabelle Von Bueltzingsloewen, *L'Hécatombe des fous: La famine dans les hôpitaux psychiatriques français sous l'Occupation* [Massacre of the Mad: Famine in French Psychiatric Hopsitals under the Occupation] (Paris: Aubier, 2007, reprinted Flammarion, "Champs Histoire." 2009).
18. Ibid., 76.
19. Tosquelles discusses his encounter with him in 1952 in François Tosquelles, "Frantz Fanon et la psychothérapie institutionnelle" [Frantz Fanon and Institutional Psychotherapy], *Sud/Nord*, vol. 22, no. 1 (2001): 71–8.
20. François Tosquelles, "Une politique de la folie," 75.
21. Patrick Faugeras and Michel Minard, "Portrait d'un militant, François Tosquelles" [François Tosquelles: Portrait of a Militant], *Sud/Nord*, vol. 25 (2010): 54.
22. Here "facility" [établissement] refers to the structure as a government-regulated body, defined above all by its internal regulations. For Tosquelles and his colleagues, everything still needed to be done to humanize it. The process of institutionalization, i.e., the creation and imple-

mentation of "structures with a disalienating function" by its very members, can subvert it. "Institution" signifies the establishment of a different kind of relationship among its members.

23. Jean Oury, "Psychothérapie institutionnelle et guerre d'Espagne: entretien avec Florent Gabarron-Garcia" [Institutional Psychotherapy and the Spanish Civil War: Interview with Florent Gabbaron-Garcia], *Chimères*, vol. 72 (2010): 11–20.

24. Frank Drogoul, "L'apport politique de Jean Oury. 'Je suis poumiste'" ["I am a poumist": Jean Oury's Political Contribution], *Figures de la psychanalyse*, vol. 33, no. 1 (2017): 156–66.

25. Jacoby, *Repression of Psychoanalysis*, 101.

26. On these questions, please refer to Danielle Papiau's political science dissertation, "Psychiatrie, psychanalyse, politique: Essai de sociobiographie des psychiatres communistes (1924–1985)" [Psychiatry, Psychoanalysis, Politics: A Sociobiographical Essay on Communist Psychiatrists], defended June 16 2017, directed by Bernard Pudal.

27. Quoted in François Dosse, *Gilles Deleuze and Félix Guattari: Intersecting Lives*, trans. Deborah Glassman (New York: Columbia University Press, 2011), 43.

28. Here, we freely draw from François Dosse's biography.

29. Jean Oury, *Il, donc* [He/It, Therefore] (Paris: Matrice, 1978), 73.

30. François Dosse, *Gilles Deleuze and Félix Guattari*, 37.

31. Claudine Dardy, Gérard Grass, Numa Murard, Georges Préli and Michel Rostain, *Histoires de La Borde, dix ans de psychothérapie institutionnelle à la clinique de Cour-Cheverny, Recherches, Revue du Cerfi*, vol. 21 (March–April 1976): 20.

32. François Dosse, *Gilles Deleuze and Félix Guattari*, 44.

33. Quoted in Jean Ayme, "Le groupe de Sèvres," *Vie social et traitements*, vol. 71 (2001): 51.

34. Félix Guattari, *Psychoanalysis and Transversality: Interviews 1955–1971*, trans. Ames Hodges (Cambridge, MA: Semiotext(e), 2015), 126–7 [trans. modified].
35. Ibid., 124.
36. It should be noted that, for some, it had no scope.
37. Later, Paul-Claude Racamier, René Diatkine, and Serge Lebovici wrote *Le Psychanalyste sans divan* [The Psychoanalyst without a Couch] (Paris: Payot, 1970).
38. Quoted in Jean Ayme, "Le groupe de Sèvres," 50.
39. Racamier et al., *Le Psychanalyste sans divan*, 68.
40. Sigmund Freud, *Group Psychology and the Analysis of the Ego*, trans. James Strachey, *Standard Edition*, vol. 18.
41. We draw freely from Robert Castel, "L'institution psychiatrique en question" [Challenging the Psychiatric in Situation], *Revue française de sociologie*, vol. 12–13 (1971): 57–92.
42. Racamier et al., *Le Psychanalyste sans divan*, 165.
43. Ibid.
44. Castel, "L'institution psychiatrique," 68.
45. Ibid., 67.
46. Guattari, *Psychoanalysis and Transversality*, 23–4.
47. Ibid., 24.
48. Ibid., 69–70.
49. Ibid., 26–7.
50. Here, a critique of the contract and the law is articulated in favor of the institutional model, as Deleuze would defend it. Ibid., 19.
51. Ibid., 90.
52. Dardy et al., *Histoires de La Borde*, 301–2. In order to distinguish the different periods of the institutional life at La Borde, please refer to this beautiful, vibrant monograph.
53. Guattari, *Psychoanalysis and Transversality*, 25. Trans. modified.
54. Deleuze and Guattari, *Anti-Oedipus*, 22.

55. Guattari, *Psychoanalysis and Transversality*, 117.
56. Ibid., 70.
57. Ibid., 109.
58. Ibid., 117.
59. Ibid.
60. With the notable and problematic exception of doctors: a symptom, it seems, that will take on catastrophic proportions with Guattari's death. The doctors then led a counterrevolution and created their own "organization [société]"—the organization of doctors: a legal and contractual system grafted onto the institution. Busy generating "certifications," like in the framework of private practice, they removed themselves from the institution. Their exceptional status (financial, imaginary, and symbolic) is all the more subjugating in institutions where all the other members are "monitors." Most psychiatrists in current institutional psychotherapy organized on this model seem to have disavowed the Marxist critique, if they even understand it at all.
61. Guattari, *Psychoanalysis and Transversality*, 16.
62. Dardy et al., *Histoires de La Borde*, 161–74.
63. Ibid., 165.
64. Ibid.
65. Guattari, *Psychoanalysis and Transversality*, 116.
66. Ibid., 108–9.
67. Ibid., 130.
68. This will be taken up with Deleuze in *Anti-Oedipus*.
69. Guattari, *Psychoanalysis and Transversality* [translation modified].
70. Ibid., 226.
71. Jacques Lacan, "The Function and Field of Speech and Language in Psychoanalysis" (1953), *Écrits*, trans. Bruce Fink (New York: W.W. Norton & Company, 2006).

72. This idea is also the subject of recent historiographic research. Against Arendt's interpretation of the "banality of evil" or historians' explanations that relativize German support for mass murder by claiming the chain of command absolves responsibility, Johann Chapoutot defends that idea that the act of killing took place "within the context of the story being told about them, and the project they were intended to advance," and that it was a "response to hopes and fears." There is a "mental universe in which Nazi crimes took place and held meaning," which allowed millions of "average" Germans (who were by no means part of the SS) to carry out and proudly take up a number of particularly atrocious acts and persecutions. This perspective recalls Reich's analysis of fascism and mass desire. Johann Chapoutot, *The Law of Blood: Thinking and Acting as a Nazi*, trans. Miranda Richmond Mouillot, (Cambridge, MA: The Belknap Press, 2018), 7–8.
73. Guattari, *Psychoanalysis and Transversality*, 227. Trans. note: the author transposes *corporéisation du groupe* here, translated further on in the Guattari as "embodying" or "corporized." He is playing on the substitutive of body, the group becoming a body itself.
74. Deleuze and Guattari, *Anti-Oedipus*, 104–5.
75. *Jacques Lacan*, "La troisième," *Lettres de l'École freudienne*, vol. 16 (1975): 177–203.
76. Here psychoanalysis identifies a series accounting for the detachable parts of the body (voice, gaze, breast, feces), i.e., that of a fragmented world where the little child does not yet have access to the representation of their own body, whose "object *a*" will bear the mark that the fantasy conceals.
77. Guattari, *Psychoanalysis and Transversality*, 227.
78. Ibid., 216.
79. Ibid., 227.

80. Ibid.
81. Jean Oury's postscript in Félix Guattari, *De Leros à La Borde* (Paris: Lignes, 2012), 89.
82. Gilles, Deleuze, "Three Group-Related Problems," in *Desert Islands and Other Texts, 1953–1974* (New York: Semiotext(e), 2002), 194.
83. Please refer to my previous book, *L'Héritage politique de la psychanalyse*.
84. Guattari, *Psychoanalysis and Transversality*, 77–8.
85. Ibid., 79.
86. Ibid., 116.
87. Ibid., 79.
88. Ibid.
89. Ibid., 117.
90. A research collective created by Guattari and several monitors working at La Borde, including authors of the monograph about La Borde.

6. Revival of Revolutionary Psychoanalysis in Germany: The Heidelberg Experience

1. Michael Tregenza, *Aktion T4: Le secret d'État des nazis—l'extermination des handicapés physiques et mentaux* [Aktion T4: The Nazi State Secret—The Extermination of the Physically and Mentally Handicapped] (Paris: Calmann-Lévy, 2011).
2. Alfred Wahl, *La seconde histoire du nazisme dans l'Allemagne fédérale de 1945* [The Second History of the Nazis in West Germany of 1945] (Paris: Armand Colin, 2006).
3. Christian Pross (in collaboration with Sonja Schweitzer and Julia Wagner), *"Wir wollten ins Verderben rennen": Die Geschichte des Sozialistischen Patienterkollektivs Heidelberg* ["We Wanted to Run to Our Doom": The History of the

Heidelberg Socialist Patients Collective] (Cologne: Psychiatrie Verlag, 2016).

4. Dossier collectif, "Les prisonniers politiques ouest-allemands accusent" [Accusations/Charges from West German Political Prisoners] *Les temps modernes*, vol. 332 (1974).
5. Félix Guattari, *La révolution moléculaire* (Paris: Les prairies ordinaires, 2012, 271).
6. Jacques Lacan, *On a Discourse That Might Not Be a Semblance: The Seminar of Jacques Lacan, Book XVIII*, trans. Bruce Fink (Cambridge: Polity Press, 2025).
7. We therefore have to address the subject's task of self-transformation as well as a transformation of the material structures on which the subject depends. Of course, Lacan does not go that far. The subject cannot be "liberated" because its alienation is above all linguistic: without semblance [*semblant*, seeming or appearance, Bruce Fink translates as imitation], it can only stray [*errer*]. Lacan only takes up the theory of fetishism by analogy in relating it to the function of language. Here, it remains within the framework of structuralist analysis. But this is not always the case.
8. SPK, *Turn Illness into a Weapon*, trans. K. D. (n.p.: n.d.), 53–4.
9. Ibid., 136n41. See also Frantz Fanon, *The Wretched of the Earth*, trans. Richard Philcox (New York: Grove Press, [1963] 2004).
10. SPK, *Turn Illness into a Weapon*, 5.
11. Ibid., 55–6.
12. Reich, *The Invasion of Compulsory Sex-Morality*. Here Reich draws on the "early Freud," for whom repression is not yet thought of in terms of an endogenous primary anxiety independent of repression.

13. Reich refers to Malinowski's well-known research: Bronislaw Malinowski, *Sex and Repression in Savage Society* (New York: Harcourt, Brace & Company, 1927).
14. SPK, *Turn Illness into a Weapon*, 56.
15. Ibid., 57, emphasis added.
16. Ibid., 57.
17. Ibid., 57.
18. Ibid., 4.
19. Ibid., 86.
20. Jean-Claude Polack, *La médecine du capital* [The Medicine of Capital] (Paris: Maspero, 1972).
21. SPK, *Turn Illness into a Weapon*, 48.
22. Ibid., 78.
23. Ibid., 46.
24. Ibid., 46–7.
25. Ibid., 46.
26. Ibid., 47.
27. Ibid., 49.
28. Ibid., 6.
29. Ibid., 68.
30. At a time when neoliberal power promotes the idea of psychiatric "rehabilitation," the SPK's perspective seems to be a burning issue.
31. Ibid., 59–60.
32. Ibid., 101.
33. Ibid., 6.
34. Ibid., 6.
35. Ibid., 44.
36. Ibid., 57, 60.
37. Ibid., 72.
38. Ibid., 68.
39. Ibid., 186–7.
40. Ibid., 73.

41. As David Cooper did in 1962 with the experiment of "Villa 21": David Cooper, *Psychiatry and Anti-Psychiatry* (London: Routledge, [1967] 2013).
42. This is what CEMEA (*Centres d'entraînement aux méthodes d'éducation active*/Active Learning Training Centers) aimed for.
43. These experiments were pioneered by Maxwell Jones, *The Therapeutic Community* (New York: Basic Books, 1953).
44. Guattari, *La révolution moléculaire*, 272. My translation.
45. SPK, *Turn Illness into a Weapon*, 52.
46. Ibid., 52.
47. Ibid., 48.
48. Guattari, *La révolution moléculaire*, 272. My translation.
49. Pross, "Wir wollten ins Verderben rennen."
50. Dossier collectif, "Le SPK, collectif socialiste de patients," *Recherches*, vol. 11 (1973): 152.
51. Dosse, *Gilles Deleuze and Félix Guattari*.
52. Collectif, *Sexualité et politique, Actes du colloque de Milan de 1975* (Paris, 10/18, 1977).
53. A precise timeline of these events can be found on the site http://www.spkpfh.de, as well in the book *Psychiatrie politique, l'affaire de Heidelberg (s.p.k)* [Political Psychiatry: The Heidelberg Case] (Paris: Maspero, 1972).
54. Dossier collectif, "Le SPK, collectif socialiste de patients," 153.

Conclusion: For Another Psychoanalysis

1. Jacoby, *Repression*, 11.
2. Elizabeth Brainin and Isidor Kaminer, "Psychanalyse et nationalsocialisme," *L'écrit du temps, Psychanalyse, moments d'histoire*, vol. 6 (1984): 59–82.

Index

port refers to a portrait

Adler, Victor 20, 78
Aichhorn, August 20, 97–9, 127
Ajuriaguerra, Julian de 140
Alexander, Franz 60, 197
Algeria 4, 176–7, 197
Almodovar del Campo 132–3
Ambulatorium Clinic 99
American Psychoanalytic Association (APA) 82
Arab Spring 8
Argentina 110–6, 124
Argentinian Federation of Psychiatry (FAP) 114
Argentinian Psychoanalytic Association (APA) 110–1, 114–7, 119, 124–5
Armand, Inès 24
Austria 62–3, 96
see also Vienna
Avellaneda Hospital 119–21

Bachofen, Johann Jakob 51
Baeyer, Walter von 170–1
Barcelona 108, 126–7
Bardach, Victor 137
Baremblitt, Gregorio 118–9

Batia, Dr. 143
Bauléo, Armando 114
Beauvoir, Simone de 191
Berlin 28, 66, 68, 90, 119
Berlin Marxist Worker's School 73
Berlin policlinic 41–2, 96, 119, 194
Berlin Psychoanalytic Institute 84–8
Bernfeld, Siegfried 20, 66, 127, 197
Bibring, Edward 105–6, 107
Bilda Hospital, Algeria 197
Boehm, Felix 86–8, 90, 92–6, 98
Bonaparte, Marie 22
Bonnafé, Lucien 138, 140
Bonneval Congress 141
Bornstein, Berta 28
Bourbaki (mathematics collective) 140
Brainin, Elisabeth 194–5
Brazil 124
Brill, Abraham A. 79*port*
British Psychoanalysis Society 82

Canguilhem, Georges 137

Casals, Pablo 127
Castel, Robert 8, 149, 191
Catalan-Balearic Communist Federation 129
Catalonia 126–30, 133–5
Catholic Youth (organization) 74
Center for Studies, Research and Institutional Training (CERFI) 168
Chestnut Lodge Clinic 197
"Children's Seminar" 41, 66
Cocks, Geoffrey 91
Commission of Relatives of Political Prisoners, Students and Trade Unions (COFAPPEG) 118–9
Communist Party of Austria 63, 101, 104
Communist Party of Germany 66–9, 71–5, 93
Communist Party of Spain 129, 134
Consultario Populare di Niguarda 197
Cordobazo movement 114–5

Daumézon, Georges 140, 143, 146
Deleuze, Gilles 153, 163–4, 191
Deleuze, Gilles and Guattari, Félix *Anti-Oedipus* 7, 166
Descartes, René 163

Deutsch, Helene 19
Diatkine, René 146–8, 150
Dreyfus-Armand, Geneviève 135

Éditions de Minuit (publisher) 137–8
Eiminder, Sándor 127
Eitingon, Max 41, 84–8, 90
Ellis, Havelock *Studies in the Psychology of Sex* 56
Éluard, Paul 137–8
Engels, Friedrich 51
Ermakoff, J. D, 80
Ey, Henri 140

Fachinelli, Elvio 114
Fanon, Frantz 4, 138, 176, 197
Federn, Paul 21, 38, 106
Fenichel, Otto 41, 61–2, 66, 84, 93–4, 96, 197
Ferenczi, Sándor 17, 19, 22, 54, 79*port*, 127
  Psychoanalysis and Education 27
Forum for Human Rights 118
Foucault, Michel 191
France 3–4, 135–40, 173, 193, 196
Frankfurt Institute of Psychoanalysis 197
Franz Josef, Emperor 102
Free Institute of Psychoanalysis 197
French Revolution 8, 15

Freud, Anna (daughter of Sigmund) 22, 28, 40, 89, 93, 96, 105
Freud, Sigmund 1−2, 4, 7, 10−22, 26, 29, 33, 35−40, 49−50, 54, 56, 64−5, 70−1, 77−82
79*port*, 86−9, 96, 105−6, 108, 148, 156, 158, 160, 194, 196
Beyond the Pleasure Principle 61
"'Civilized' Sexual Morality and Modern Nervous Illness" 65
Civilization and its Discontents 10, 12−13, 65, 77−8, 80−2
Future of an Illusion, The 12−13, 32−3, 77, 79, 81
Group Psychology and Analysis of the Ego 51
Outline of Psychoanalysis, An 164
Question of a Weltanschauung, The 84, 89
Three Essays on Sexuality 35
Fröbel, Friedrich 27
Fromm, Erich 20, 66, 197
Fromm-Reichmann, Frieda 197
Furet, François 8

Georgette (monitor at La Borde) 155−6

German Association for Proletarian Sexual Politics (Sexpol) 71−2, 74−5, 76, 89
German Institute for Psychological Research and Psychotherapy 95
German Institute of Psychotherapy 96
German Journal of Psychoanalysis on the Soil of the Third Reich 96−7
German Psychoanalytic Association 89
German Psychoanalytic Institute 9, 96
German Psychoanalytic Society 89−92, 94−8, 195
German Society for General Medicine 91−2
Germany *see* Berlin; Frankfurt; Heidelberg; Nazism
Gévaudan Society 138
Goebbels, Joseph 162
Göring, Matthias 95, 96, 98
Göring Institute 96−7, 124, 194−5
Gramsci, Antonio 119
Grinberg, Léon 112
Gruppo Milanese per lo sviluppo della psicoterapia 114
Guattari, Félix 7, 128, 139, 142−5, 147, 150, 152−4, 157−61, 159*port*, 163−7,

170, 173, 186–7, 189, 191, 196

Hall, G. Stanley 79*port*
Heidelberg 3, 169–71, 189–92
Hindenberg, Paul von 75
Hitler, Adolf 69, 84, 163
  Mein Kampf 91
Hitler Youth (organization) 74
Hobbes, Thomas 10, 81
Huber, Dr. Wolfgang 170–2, 171*port*, 189–91
Hug-Hellmuth, Hermine 28
Hungary 19, 22

Ibárruri, Dolores (*La Pasionaria*) 109
Iberian Anarchist Federation (FAI) 129
International Brigades 108, 113, 126, 134–5
International Congress of Psychoanalysis
  (1918) 11
  (1934) 92
International Psychoanalytic Association (IPA) 26, 37–8, 82, 84, 92–5, 97–8, 114, 116, 124, 195
  Congress (1922) 39
  Congress (1934) 92
  Congress (1938) 97–8

Jacobson, Edith 93–5, 107
Jacoby, Russell 193

Jensen, Fritz 101
Jenotdel (women's section of Russian Communist Party) 24
Jones, Ernest 10–11, 22, 79*port*, 82–6, 92–3, 96–8, 107–8, 128, 194, 195–6
  The Life and Work of Freud 82–3
Jung, Carl 2, 79*port*

Kaminer, Isidor 194–5
Kamm, Bernhard 94
Kemper, Werner 90, 95, 124
Kenstemberg, Evelyne 143
Kinderheim Baumgarten, Berlin 28
Kingsley Hall 197
Klein, Melanie 26–30, 111–2
Kollontaï, Alexandra 24, 103

La Borde Clinic 3, 128, 138–9, 142–7, 150–6, 168
Lacan, Jacques 140–7, 156, 160–1, 163–6, 173
Laforgue, René 61
Laing, R. D. 197
Landauer, Karl 20
Langer, Marie 100–25, 104*port*, 140
  Group Psychotherapy 112–13
  Maternity and Sex 111, 113
Langer, Veronica (daughter of Marie) 108, 112–13
Lawyers' Union 119

Le Bon, Gustave 160
Le Guillant, Louis 140, 143
Lenin, V. I. 23, 28–9, 68, 80
Libros, Los (magazine) 115–6
Linden, Herbert 96
Lukács, György 19
Luxemburg, Rosa 19

Mao, Zedong 119
Marx, Karl and Marxism 25, 51–2, 73, 89–90, 105, 119, 161, 169, 172–4, 179
Matarasso, Henri 137
#MeToo movement 5
Mitchell, Juliet 113
Montseny, Federica 109
Moreira, Amilcar Lobo 124–5
Morgan, Lewis Henry 51
Moscow Institute 80
Müller-Braunschweig, Carl 86, 88, 90–1, 94–8

National Confederation of Labor (CNT) 128–9
National Socialist German Workers' Party (Nazi Party) 66–7, 95
Nazism 62, 66–9, 75, 88–9, 95, 169, 174, 183, 194–5
Negrín, Juan 134
New Philosophers movement 6–7, 8
New Russian Psychoanalytic Bookshop 25–6
Nicaragua 125

Nitzsche, Bernd 94, 98

Orwell, George 108–9, 127
Oury, Jean 128, 139, 140–5, 141*port*, 147, 150–3, 166
Oury, Fernand (brother of Jean) 142

Pain, François 138
Pankow, Gisela 141*port*
Pappenheim, Martin 25
Paris Commune (1871) 189
Pavlovsky, Eduardo 118–9
Péron, Juan 110
Pfister, Oskar 13, 15
Plataforma Argentina 115–8
Plataforma Internacional 114–5
Political Psychology and Sex Economy Review 76
Polack, Jean-Claude 138, 181, 184
Populaire (newspaper) 135
Primo de Rivera, Miguel 128, 130
Pross, Christian 171–2
Psychoanalytic Pedagogy (journal) 20
Psychoanalytic Labaoratory, Vincennes 197

Racamier, Paul-Claude 144, 146–9, 151, 154, 156
Recherches (magazine) 191–2
Red Orchestra Network 96

Reich, Annie (wife of Wilhelm)
  Adults' Secrets Revealed to Children 74
  When Your Child Asks Questions 74
Reich, Wilhelm 1–2, 7, 15, 20, 34–76, 38*port*, 83–4, 115, 119–21, 172–5, 177, 195, 196
  "The Concepts of Instinct and Libido from Forel to Jung" 35
  Impulsive Character, The 42
  Invasion of Compulsory Sexual Morality, The 74, 177–8
  Mass Psychology of Fascism 67, 89, 92
  "On 'Genitality' from the Standpoint of Psychoanalytic Prognosis and Therapy" 38–9
  Sexual Maturity, Abstinence, Marital Morals 65
  Sexual Struggle of Youth, The 74, 76
  What is Class Consciousness? 72–3
Reichswart (newspaper) 91
Reik, Theodor 60–1
Rickman, John 98
Rittmeister, John 95–6
Rodrigué, Emilio 112, 114, 116
Rosenthal, Tatiana 25
Rothschild, Berthold 114
Russia 13, 15–17, 22–9, 62–4, 79–80
  see also Moscow
Russian Society of Psychoanalysis 26–7

Saint-Alban Hospital 2, 136–41
Sandinista National Liberation Front 125
Sartre, Jean-Paul 175, 191
Saumery Clinic 142
Schmidt, Vera 1, 27, 28*port*, 29–33, 80
Schober, Johann 62
Schopenhauer, Arthur 103
Schwarzwald Schule 103
Second International 20
Sept-Fons refugee camp 135–6
Sèvres Group 143–4, 146–7, 154–5
Shultz-Hencke, Harald 88
Sicadon, Danièle 138
Simmel, Ernst 19, 84
  Psychoanalysis of the Masses 21–2
Social Democratic Worker's Party, Austria 20
Socialist Patients Collective (SPK) 3, 169–72, 171*ports*, 174–7, 179–81, 183–91

Socialist Society for Sexual Counseling and Sexology 54
Society of Socialist Doctors 19
Spanish Civil War 108–10, 126–39
 see also Barcelona; Catalonia; International Brigades
Spazier, Dr. 170
Spiegel, Der 190
Spielrein, Sabina 80
Stalin, Joseph 33, 64, 80, 101, 129–30, 133–4, 174
State Psychoanalytic Institute, Russia 22, 25
Sterba, Richard 37–8, 64–5, 97, 105–6, 108

Tandler, Julius 21, 35
Teaching and Research Centers, Argentina 115
Tosquelles, François 2–3, 109, 126–33, 140, 141*port*, 142, 144, 147
Trait d'Union (newspaper) 139
Trotsky, Leon 20
Turn Illness into a Weapon (SPK) 175
Tzara, Tristan 137

United States 140, 193, 197

Vienna 17, 20–1, 34, 41–2, 50–2, 57–60, 62
 Red Vienna 21, 100–1, 109
Vienna Psychoanalytic Society 25, 35, 97, 105–7, 110

Workers' International Relief (organization) 51
Worker's Party of Marxist Unification (POUM) 109, 131, 133–4, 139
World League for Sexual Reform 71
Wulff, Mosche 80

Zadniker (friend of Reich) 53–4
Zentralblatt für Psychotherapie 91
Zetkin, Clara 23

The Pluto Press Newsletter

Hello friend of Pluto!

Want to stay on top of the best radical books we publish?

Then sign up to be the first to hear about our new books, as well as special events, podcasts and videos.

You'll also get 50% off your first order with us when you sign up.

Come and join us!

Go to bit.ly/PlutoNewsletter